A SPECIAL CHILD IN THE FAMILY
Living with your sick or disabled child

DIANA KIMPTON was already interested in the problems of disabled children when she found that her own two boys had cystic fibrosis. Since then her interest has grown and developed and, as well as caring for her own special children, she has helped with Riding for the Disabled and provided respite care for a brain-damaged child.

Overcoming Common Problems Series

The ABC of Eating
Coping with anorexia, bulimia and
compulsive eating
JOY MELVILLE

Beating the Blues
SUSAN TANNER AND JILLIAN
BALL

Beating Job Burnout
DR DONALD SCOTT

Being the Boss
STEPHEN FITZSIMON

Birth Over Thirty
SHEILA KITZINGER

Body Language
How to read others' thoughts by their
gestures
ALLAN PEASE

Bodypower
DR VERNON COLEMAN

Calm Down
How to cope with frustration and anger
DR PAUL HAUCK

Comfort for Depression
JANET HORWOOD

Common Childhood Illnesses
DR PATRICIA GILBERT

Complete Public Speaker
GYLES BRANDRETH

Coping with Anxiety and Depression
SHIRLEY TRICKETT

Coping with Cot Death
SARAH MURPHY

Coping with Depression and Elation
DR PATRICK McKEON

Coping with Stress
DR GEORGIA WITKIN-LANOIL

Coping with Suicide
DR DONALD SCOTT

Coping with Thrush
CAROLINE CLAYTON

**Coping Successfully with Your Child's
Asthma**
DR PAUL CARSON

**Coping Successfully with Your Child's Skin
Problems**
DR PAUL CARSON

**Coping Successfully with Your Hyperactive
Child**
DR PAUL CARSON

Coping Successfully with Your Irritable Bowel
ROSEMARY NICOL

Curing Arthritis Diet Book
MARGARET HILLS

Curing Arthritis – The Drug-free Way
MARGARET HILLS

**Curing Coughs, Colds and Flu – the
Drug-free Way**
MARGARET HILLS

Curing Illness – The Drug-free Way
MARGARET HILLS

Depression
DR PAUL HAUCK

Divorce and Separation
ANGELA WILLANS

The Dr Moerman Cancer Diet
RUTH JOCHEMS

The Epilepsy Handbook
SHELAGH McGOVERN

**Everything You Need to Know about
Adoption**
MAGGIE JONES

**Everything You Need to Know about
Contact Lenses**
DR ROBERT YOUNGSON

**Everything You Need to Know about Your
Eyes**
DR ROBERT YOUNGSON

**Everything You Need to Know about the
Pill**
WENDY COOPER AND TOM SMITH

Everything You Need to Know about Shingles
DR ROBERT YOUNGSON

Family First Aid and Emergency Handbook
DR ANDREW STANWAY

Feverfew
A traditional herbal remedy for migraine
and arthritis
DR STEWART JOHNSON

Fight Your Phobia and Win
DAVID LEWIS

Overcoming Common Problems Series

Overcoming Common Problems Series

Overcoming Common Problems

A SPECIAL CHILD
IN THE FAMILY

Living with your sick or disabled child

Diana Kimpton

SHELDON PRESS

LONDON

First published in Great Britain 1990
Sheldon Press, SPCK, Marylebone Road, London NW1 4DU

British Library Cataloguing in Publication Data
Kimpton, Diana
   A special child in the family: living with your sick or disabled child. –
(Overcoming common problems).
   1. Great Britain. Handicapped children. Care.
Participation of parents
   I. Title II. Series
   362.7

ISBN 0–85969–607–3

          Typeset by Deltatype Ltd, Ellesmere Port, South Wirral
      Printed in Great Britain by Biddles Ltd, Guildford and Kings Lynn

To Rachel Carter and Cathy Dean

Contents

CONTENTS

Acknowledgements

So many people have helped with this book that it is impossible to name them all here. My thanks go to all the parents who have shared their feelings and their experiences, and to the professionals who so willingly have spared the time to explain about their jobs. I have been overwhelmed by the assistance I have received – no one I approached refused to help.

Writing a book is a long, slow task. I would never have succeeded without the encouragement of my family, especially Steve who has carried out the essential task of telling me when I was writing rubbish. Special thanks are also due to April Barry, Jill Cooper, Ed Griffiths, Cynthia Naylor, Claire Sharp, Sheila Wolfendale and the Advisory Centre for Education for commenting on parts of the first draft.

I am very grateful to Jack Ashley MP and Lenore Hill for allowing me to quote their advice. My thanks also go to Professor Sheila Wolfendale for permitting me to include the Guidelines for Parents in Chapter 27.

Introduction

If your child is handicapped, disabled or sick, this book is for you. The exact diagnosis does not matter, for the problems, worries and fears covered here are those common to all parents in your situation.

This is the book I searched for in vain when I learnt my own two boys were incurably ill with cystic fibrosis. I was frightened of my own emotions and I needed to know that it was alright to feel so bad. I needed a book written *for* parents rather than about them, a book which did not just list the problems I was having but also suggested ways I could improve matters. In the end, I gave up looking and decided to write it myself. This is the result.

This book is about feelings and how to cope with them; it is about the help available and how to get the best from it; it is about the great taboos that no one talks about, like death and failing to cope.

The ideas in here are parent-size ones you can try yourself. They are based on people's practical experiences, not vague theory. Remember, they are only suggestions not rules: don't feel you must follow them all slavishly but instead use them as starting points for your own solutions.

Sadly, the English language lacks one word to stand instead of 'he' or 'she'. The modern alternatives of s/he or she/he do not fit easily into my style of writing so I have chosen to use 'he' for your child and 'she' for the professionals. If necessary, please substitute the appropriate words as you read.

PART ONE
Early Days

1

First Shock

To be told there is something seriously wrong with your child must be one of the most devastating events any person can experience. If it has happened to you, don't be upset by the strength of your reactions for they are perfectly justifiable. Suddenly, the hopes and dreams you had for your child are gone, to be replaced by an uncertain future full of problems. Nothing will ever be the same again. It is natural for you to go through an emotional turmoil in the days and weeks following your child's diagnosis as you adjust to this new reality.

Sometimes your feelings may be so intense that you fear you cannot cope with them. You may even worry you are going mad. Don't despair. Other people have trodden this path before, feeling just as bad. They survived and so will you. To help you see how normal you are, let's consider some of the most common reactions parents feel.

I don't want him

Three weeks after our younger son was born, we were told he had cystic fibrosis. Travelling home with him, I suddenly felt an almost instinctive urge to leave him on the bus, to go home without him and lead a life free of the complications he had brought with him. Fortunately that feeling lasted only a moment. I pushed it away as soon as it came for I already loved my baby too much to abandon him. However, that brief moment has left me with great sympathy for any mother who finds it hard to accept her handicapped baby.

Perhaps you feel you don't want this new child. After all, you've just spent nine months awaiting the arrival of a perfect baby. This one is not perfect so he does not feel like yours.

I expect you are frightened too: frightened of all the problems that lie ahead, frightened of how other people will react. Perhaps you are even frightened of the baby himself, especially if you have not seen him yet and you know he will look different. On top of everything else, you are probably frightened by your own reactions, by your own fear.

The best cure for all these feelings is your baby. Look at him and, if possible, hold him. This may not be easy if he has been rushed to a

5

special care unit, perhaps even one in a different hospital. However, babies in incubators can usually be touched even if they cannot be cuddled. If you are very frightened of seeing your child or cannot do so because of distance or your health, ask someone to take some photographs for you. Otherwise the pictures produced by your imagination will be far worse than reality.

Your feelings of rejection may vanish when you see your baby, or it may take weeks or months of caring for him before they go. Be patient with yourself. Many mothers of ordinary babies find it takes time for their love to grow. You may need time to adjust before you can see your child as a baby who happens to have a problem rather than a problem who happens to be a baby.

It is particularly tempting to reject a baby who is going to die. It seems less painful to abandon him now than to let your love grow, only to suffer the heartache of losing him later. Caring for a dying child is a great emotional strain but so is living with the knowledge that you turned your back on a child who needed you.

It may be, in the end, that you still feel unable to cope with this baby. If so, please take an active interest in his future. All children have a right to be loved, however handicapped or sick they may be, and however short their lives. Adoptive and foster homes are now found for even very severely handicapped or dying children. Please don't deny your child the opportunity of being part of a happy family just because it would make you feel uncomfortable to see someone else cope with a situation you could not manage yourself. Remember their circumstances may be different from yours so it might be easier for them to cope. If you can bring yourselves to do so, meet his new parents. Hopefully you will then feel more relaxed about his future and, in time, he may know that you gave him up in love rather than running from him in fear.

I wish he were dead

After you have been told your child has serious problems, the future looks bleak and scary. Your hopes and dreams have been destroyed so you can only see difficulties ahead. Perhaps you are thinking, 'If only he'd die now. Then we could grieve for him, get over it and go on as we were before.' It's easy to think like that, especially if your child is very frail or is likely to die young anyway. You feel trapped by this disaster and the death of your child seems a way of escape.

Entertaining such thoughts, even momentarily, can leave you

riddled with guilt that you don't love your baby. That is being very hard on yourself. Many parents feel like that at first but such feelings usually pass as you get to know your baby and grow to love him. The future is rarely so black as you imagine it in those early days.

The situation is more complicated if you are asked to make life-or-death decisions for your new baby, such as granting consent for life-saving surgery which will still leave him handicapped afterwards. You are still suffering from the shock of diagnosis and are probably finding it difficult to make even small decisions like what to give your family for breakfast so it is hardly surprising that making such a momentous decision is especially hard for you. Try to think of what is best for your baby, not what is convenient for you. No child should be allowed to die just because his parents don't want him. Never be afraid to ask for more information or a second opinion if time allows.

Very, very occasionally the idea that your child would be better off dead stays and grows until you seriously consider helping him on his way. *DON'T DO IT!* Talk to someone about how you feel instead, someone you feel safe confiding in. Try a trusted friend, your doctor, health visitor or another parent. If you would feel more comfortable talking to a stranger, phone your local NSPCC inspector or one of the helplines for parents under stress. (see Appendix A)

It's such a relief to know

Many problems are not noticeable at birth but only develop or become noticeable as your child grows older. If this is your situation, it is likely you were the first to suspect something was wrong. Perhaps you noticed differences between your child and his brothers and sisters or between him and your friends' children. Alternatively, you may have spotted the first signs of an undiagnosed progressive disease. You may have been lucky and had those early worries explained quickly.

It is more likely, though, that your initial concerns were followed by a long period of uncertainty. Perhaps your GP or health visitor took no notice of your worries, believing you to be an over-anxious mother. But, even if everyone agreed something was wrong, it may have taken months before a proper diagnosis was made.

If this has happened to you, one of your first reactions to the diagnosis may be relief. You are no longer a fussy mother who worries about nothing. No longer can anyone suggest (however subtly) that it is your fault your child is not growing or learning properly. Now you have a label to help you explain why your child's behaviour is strange or his speech poor.

You may feel guilty that such bad news should produce a reaction even remotely like pleasure. Don't condemn yourself. Why shouldn't you feel relief when you have been released from uncertainty? Only now you know what you are facing can you start working out how to cope with it.

I'm so depressed I can't stop crying

This is probably the most common reaction of all – I have a file full of letters to prove it. This is not a depressive illness coming for no reason but a perfectly normal reaction to a devastating event. Your plans and expectations for the future are shattered so you need to grieve for them before you can pick up the pieces of your new life.

Don't feel a freak for crying. You have every right to cry, and it's good for you. Crying releases the tensions and pain, and helps you work through your grief.

Friends and relatives who are upset at seeing you so unhappy may urge you to ask your doctor for sedatives or antidepressants. Try to manage without them if you can (except as a short-term measure if you hit a really bad patch). Sometimes just talking to your doctor can help without her needing to prescribe anything.

Alcohol is an obvious alternative to prescribed drugs, but drowning your sorrows in a bottle of scotch provides only temporary relief. Remember tomorrow you will still have all your problems plus a hangover and if you continue to drink heavily you will just add to your family's difficulties.

Eventually your depression will lift and you will stop crying. In the meantime, share your feelings with your partner rather than turning inwards on yourself. You could also try talking to a friend who is a good listener or to another parent whose child has problems. Don't worry if you cry while you are talking. There is no shame in crying.

Looking for something positive in your life can help you feel less depressed. I know it is difficult but try to concentrate on what your child can do rather than on what he can't. If the future looks scary, try concentrating on today rather than tomorrow. Cultivate the knack of not looking too far ahead.

Learning exercises and other ways of helping your child can make you feel more in control of what happens. You may also feel depressed by the thought of all the extra work or frightened of the responsibility of carrying out treatments. All three reactions are equally normal and you may well find you have all of them in turns according to how good or bad you are feeling.

I am so angry

Anger is another way to release the tensions that build up inside you. You may both find you lose your temper more easily. Little things which would not have bothered you before may now drive you to distraction. You explode at unsuspecting shop assistants and repair men. You kick the washing machine when it breaks down and may well find you are swearing more than usual. Sadly, you may also shout at your partner and your other children.

Some of your anger may be more directed to its source. Perhaps you are angry with the doctors for not spotting the problem sooner or with God for letting such a bad thing happen.

Anger is a difficult emotion to handle. It can sow seeds of hate. It can eat away at you and make you bitter or lead you to say hurtful things you later regret. An outburst of anger can hurt a good friendship so badly that it takes a long time to heal.

Try to work off your anger without hurting anyone. Dig the garden, scrub the floor, punch a cushion, kick a football or just go off by yourself and scream or have a good cry. Laughter can be a great help. It diffuses anger, relaxing its grip on you. Time spent watching comedies on TV or reading funny books can be time well spent.

If your anger is directed against someone like a doctor or an unsympathetic relative, try writing a letter. Put into it all your rage and hurt. Make it as abusive as you want. Then tear it up and throw it away. That may sound like a strange idea but it is surprisingly effective. If there is a specific cause for your anger, you will deal with it better when you have calmed down.

Finally, if you really do lose your temper with someone, don't forget to say 'I'm sorry'.

It must have been my fault

It is very common to feel guilty that somehow you caused your child's problems. Perhaps the condition is inherited from both of you so you start thinking 'I should have married someone else'. Perhaps no one knows why your child is like he is but you worry it is because you took some medicine while you were pregnant or you kept on smoking.

The worst situation is when you know for certain things could have been different. If you had closed the gate or seen the car coming, the accident might never have happened; if you had called the doctor earlier, the complications might never have developed.

Life is full of 'what if's and 'might have been's. Sadly, no amount of worry or regret will change what has already happened. You need to put the past behind you and concentrate on today. I know that this is much easier to say than to do but you can at least make a start. Try not to punish yourself, thinking how good things could have been. If you start to do it, make a conscious effort to stop. Having company around can help here as can any activity which occupies your mind.

If your child's problems could have been avoided or minimized by your actions or someone else's, you may want to do something to prevent other children suffering in the same way. As well as helping others, this may also ease your feelings of guilt. However, don't be surprised if you cannot cope with doing anything about it until you are more accustomed to your new reality. Perhaps someone a little more removed from the situation could start things moving if you feel immediate action is needed such as an official complaint to the Health Authority or a campaign for a pedestrian crossing.

I feel such a failure.
I'm jealous of other people's babies

Most people produce ordinary, healthy babies so it is not surprising if you feel a failure for having a child who is not quite perfect. This effect is more pronounced if this is your first baby than if you have had other healthy children already. It can leave you with a great desire for another child even if the doctors advise against it.

It is hard to see someone else enjoying what you don't have, to see someone else succeed where you have failed. It can rekindle old hurts, rubbing salt into wounds you thought had healed. It was several years after Matthew was born before I could feel real joy at the birth of a friend's baby without any twinges of jealousy. Such feelings are only natural and very common but they do grow less as time goes on.

You may find visits to the baby clinic particularly difficult. Seeing other babies growing and developing can be a painful reminder that your child is different. The comments and reactions of the other mothers can also be difficult to handle when you are feeling so vulnerable. Talk to your health visitor to see if she could help make things easier. Perhaps she could visit you at home sometimes or she could help explain your baby's difficulties to the other mothers. It may not even be necessary for you to visit the clinic regularly if your doctor is already monitoring your child's progress.

Will I always feel this bad?

The straight answer to that is 'No'. Life will look better as time goes by. Even if the situation does not improve, you will adjust to it.

Gradually you will feel better emotionally but don't be surprised if the progress is not very smooth. Helping your child's progress with physiotherapy can fill you with hope only to have the old despair return later because of an unthinking comment from a stranger.

The bad times do not last forever but neither do they vanish overnight. Most parents I have contacted felt it was between 18 months and two-and-a-half years before they had come to terms with the situation fully and life had settled into its new normality.

Once you feel more settled, don't despair if the old emotions come flooding back occasionally, perhaps triggered by a change in your situation. Explaining your child's problems to the teachers in his new school can have this effect, as can seeing new signs of deterioration when your child has a progressive disease. This is a normal reaction so don't feel you are cracking under the strain.

Having a child with special needs is not something you get over but you do get used to it. You will never again be the person you were before but that is not necessarily a bad thing. Just as a useless lump of clay is turned into a useful cup by moulding and fire, so trouble can change us into better, stronger people if we let it.

2

Finding out More

I don't know how you were given your child's diagnosis. Perhaps the doctor bluntly told you the basic facts and nothing else. Maybe you were more fortunate and were given time, consideration and a sympathetic explanation of what was wrong. Whichever way it was for you, two apparently contradictory facts hold true.

First, you will remember that moment for the rest of your life. Little details like a crack in the wall or the way the doctor fiddled with his pen will remain indelibly printed in your mind.

Second, much of the actual information will have failed to sink in, especially anything offered after you were actually told the diagnosis. One mum spent a whole hour listening to a full explanation of her son's temporal epilepsy from a very considerate doctor. But when she related the visit to her husband, all she could remember was the name of the condition and the fact that he might have to go to a special school. You may have fared better but the chances are that only the basic diagnosis and a few disjointed facts have sunk into your brain. Perhaps a short phrase like 'He'll never walk' or 'She'll die before she's five' dances round your head in confusion without you fully remembering the reasons why.

This situation is almost universal. It is only after the appointment is over and the shock has worn off that questions flood into your mind, questions which must be answered if you are to understand your child's problems fully.

The professionals

Obviously your consultant is a good source of information. He should understand your difficulties so he won't be surprised if you need him to repeat his explanations several times. Don't hesitate to ask questions for fear of looking stupid.

Your GP and your health visitor are also possible sources of information but, remember, they are not specialists. If this is the first time they have met your child's particular condition, they may not be able to answer all your questions straight away. However, they should be able to find out the answers.

Voluntary groups and societies

There is a wide range of voluntary societies working on behalf of children with special needs. They vary widely in size and in the help they offer but they are all good at providing basic information. Contact any which seem to cover your child's problems. There are some addresses at the end of this book but you can find others in your local library or the *Disability Rights Handbook*. If your child's condition is very rare, there may be no society for it as yet. However, some of the wider-ranging organizations like MENCAP or I CAN may be able to help or suggest another group which can.

Many societies publish regular newsletters which can keep you up-to-date on the latest developments in treatment and on welfare issues. They are usually willing to put you in touch with other families and some operate networks of parents willing to support others through the early stages after diagnosis. Keeping in touch with the relevant voluntary society for your child's condition can stop you feeling too isolated.

Books

I hardly need to suggest books as a source of information – you must have already thought of them or you wouldn't be reading this one! But I just want to warn you not to fall into the same trap I did.

When my elder son, Paul, was diagnosed my instant reaction was to go to the library for more information. I was heart-broken when the first book declared that all cystic fibrosis children died before they were two. I looked at my apparently healthy 16-month-old toddler in despair. Why hadn't the doctor told us how little time was left? Fortunately I glanced at the date of publication. The book was twenty years old, dating back to the time when treatment was virtually non-existent. The real situation was much better and improving all the time.

I'm not saying it's not worth reading old books – just remember they may paint an unnecessarily gloomy picture for the treatment and education of special children has improved enormously over recent years. Of course, people are the same as they always were so a description of how someone felt in your situation will still be relevant even if it is rather old.

Other parents

Other parents with children similar to your own are an excellent source of support and information. It is good to chat to someone who you know understands how you feel. As well as helping you understand what the doctors have said, parents in a situation similar to your own will often have sensible ideas on overcoming practical problems. They may have ways to make physiotherapy more fun, ideas on making a boring diet more interesting or tips on how to get your child to swallow his medicine. If their children are older, they can let you see what the future may really hold, which may not be as gloomy as you had imagined.

Talking to local parents of special children can make you feel less isolated even if their children's problems are not exactly the same as yours. They will also have useful information about the support services and schools in your area.

If your voluntary society or local DIAL group cannot put you in touch with other parents, try 'Contact a Family' or 'In Touch' who both exist primarily to link parents together. Your health visitor or social worker may also be able to arrange local contacts for you. Ask them if there is a local toy library or mother-and-toddler group for special-needs children as both provide a meeting place for parents as well as company for your child.

Conflicting information

As you contact people and read books, you may receive conflicting information from the different sources. Research is continuing all the time and you are learning about the frontiers of medical knowledge. Some of what you read will be opinion and theory rather than proven fact. But without different people having different ideas, no progress would be made, for it is by testing these theories that knowledge grows and treatments improve.

Although that explains why opinions vary, it won't stop you worrying that your child is not receiving the best possible care. If you hear of a different treatment you would like to try, talk about it with the professionals working with your child. They may persuade you of their reasons for not using it or they may be willing to try it. If not, you can ask for a referral to a clinic that does use it.

Alternative medicine

Orthodox medicine does not have a monopoly on ideas for treating sick and handicapped children. You may come across some which involve alternative (or complementary) medicine. Such ideas can sound very tempting, especially if ordinary doctors have little or nothing to offer.

You will usually have to pay for alternative medicine. Most practitioners are responsible people but, as in most jobs, there are some who are not. Beware of any treatment which could be potentially harmful and of suggestions you should stop giving your child vital drugs. Remember, the ultimate responsibility is yours – don't be talked into a treatment you are unsure about. You could ask your ordinary doctor's opinion as well.

If you want to try alternative medicine, look for a qualified practitioner who is registered with the governing body of his particular field. Ideally, go to one recommended by someone else who has been successfully treated for a similar problem.

And finally

Learning about your child's problems may seem a daunting task at first. Professionals and other more experienced parents use words you don't understand. I remember when my husband Steve first went to a cystic fibrosis (CF) parents meeting, he came home amazed at the ease with which other parents used names for infections and drugs which he could hardly pronounce. Don't give up; like us, you'll get there in the end. Admit when you don't understand what people are saying and ask for an explanation; they won't laugh at you.

It is important that you understand your child's condition as much as you can. You are the people who love and care for him. The professionals may come and go but you, hopefully, will be with him right through his childhood. The more you understand, the better you can help him.

15

PART TWO
The Professionals

3

Getting Along

Whatever your child's problem, there will be professionals involved with his care. Your contact with them can be very useful but may also be stressful. Meeting them reaffirms that your child is different, reawakening the emotions which you thought you had under control. As a result, it is only natural that you should be super-sensitive to any real or imagined lack of understanding on their parts, especially in the early months after diagnosis. I know I have shed many tears in hospital car parks and at home, after putting on a brave face during the actual appointments.

The professionals you see will each have some special skill to offer. They will have been trained in their specific area of knowledge but will sometimes have had little or no training on how to get on with people or on how parents and children feel. The best ones work it out for themselves and are both understanding and approachable. The others may add to your problems by giving poor explanations, making you feel ignorant or just being brusque and offhand. This is often due to shyness or lack of understanding rather than plain nastiness.

Everyone has their good and bad days. Working with sick and handicapped children does not protect people from indigestion, troubles at home or plain exhaustion. Sometimes even the most caring professional may need to draw back, to give a little less of herself than usual. I am not trying to excuse all rudeness and bad behaviour, but just pointing out that sometimes there are extenuating circumstances, so don't condemn someone too quickly or assume a change in attitude is your fault.

Getting along

If you have read *What Katy Did* by Susan Coolidge, you may remember Cousin Helen's advice about everyone being like a box with two handles, a rough one and a smooth one. If you take the rough handle, the box is very difficult to carry but if you take the smooth one you can carry it easily.

Although the book is quite old now, the advice is still good. You receive a far better response from people if you are pleasant to them. It costs nothing to be friendly and smiles are much more

19

effective than scowls. I know this is difficult advice to follow when you have just spent two hours in a crowded waiting room with a fractious toddler, but there is nothing to be gained by starting an interview in a bad temper.

I don't mean you should always be a doormat; far from it! The art is to be assertive rather than aggressive. If you are still unsure of something when the person you are visiting starts signalling the end of the interview (by closing your file or giving the next appointment date), don't take the hint. Just stay put, smile pleasantly and ask for another explanation, demonstration or whatever you need. Don't feel guilty about asking for a little more time. Another few minutes then can save you hours of worry later or prevent you making mistakes with your child's treatment.

Although smiling is usually better than shouting, it is not always better than crying. It is possible to put on such a brave face that everyone thinks you are coping well without realizing how tough life becomes at times. Although I am not recommending crocodile tears, no one will think badly of you if you cry.

A few tears may have more effect by showing how much you need help than any amount of words. Lowering your own emotional defences enough to cry may even help break down the barriers between you and the professional concerned. As one self-professed bureaucrat told me, 'It is difficult to keep up an act when faced with someone crying. Tears can help break up a them/us attitude and replace it with a partnership.'

Personalities matter

No professional approach is right for all parents. A social worker may seem strong and decisive to one parent while another feels she is bossy and overbearing. One family may be delighted when their doctor discusses the choice of treatment with them while another may find the same approach threatening as it makes them feel responsible for the decisions made.

If you meet a professional whose approach or personality you do not like, it is sometimes possible to change. To make sure you don't opt for someone worse, find out about the alternatives before you take any action by asking other parents or professionals. In the end, you may decide to put up with a difficult relationship if the help that person offers is the best available. In other words, you may cope better with a brusque, offhand manner from the top specialist in your child's condition than you would with the same attitude from an inexperienced social worker.

Easing the stress

The large number of professionals involved with your child can cause problems in just fitting in all the visits. You run out of time and energy eventually and fares can be a problem, especially if Mum and/or Dad is losing pay to attend appointments.

Each individual professional is only aware of the contact she has with you. Only you will know if this is the fifth appointment this week or that your child is tired of being prodded and poked. If you find things are getting too much, say so and give yourselves a rest. I usually choose to ditch school medicals and routine dental appointments but your priorities may be different. Don't forget to tell them you are not coming so the appointment can be given to someone else.

Communication problems

Another difficulty which arises from the number of people involved is communication or, more precisely, the lack of it. You may be in contact with professionals from several departments – perhaps social services, education and the health authority – each of which is a separate organization with separate finance. But your child's needs overlap these departmental boundaries.

Some professionals may recommend help which they cannot provide. For example, a social worker or doctor may offer opinions on suitable schools although such decisions are really the field of the education department. If someone recommends particular help for your child, ask if they are in a position to organize its provision. If they can't, ask who can.

One method of communication used by some professionals (especially non-medical ones like social workers and education specialists) is the case conference. This brings together various professionals connected with your child so joint plans and decisions can be made. Sometimes parents are included too, so if you know one is to be held, ask if you can attend. You can also suggest that a case conference be held if you are worried the experts are not communicating with each other. You may not get the meeting but just asking for it should tell everyone a problem exists.

If you do attend a case conference, you may find it rather daunting. The other people present will probably know each other as well as having the confidence of experience and professional expertise. You will only know them through their involvement with your child and some people may be strangers. You will also be the only one present who is emotionally involved. It can help if both Mum and Dad go as you will feel less outnumbered. Don't be afraid to take some notes with you such as a list of points you want discussed, dates of absence from school or anything else you feel is relevant.

Clinic visits

Nearly all visits to clinics involve waiting around for ages. Time allowed for appointments is rarely long enough so the delays worsen as the session progresses. If you have a choice, always opt for an early appointment unless it would involve you in a mad rush to get there on time.

Incidentally, a phenomenon called 'Sod's Law' operates at clinics. I discovered it the only time we ever wandered into Outpatients fifteen minutes late. The waiting room was deserted except for two nurses and a consultant who were wondering where we were. Remember, the day you don't arrive on time because they always run late is the day they won't.

Always go to clinics expecting to be kept waiting. Arm yourself with spare nappies, feeds, colouring books and whatever is appropriate to your family. If you are seen straight away, you will be so pleased that you won't mind having dragged all that unnecessary clutter with you.

If your child is particularly difficult to entertain and the waiting room is bulging, ask for a rough idea of how long you will have to wait. Then you can go away to get a drink or find a place where shouting, screaming and running about attract less attention. Don't forget to tell someone you will be coming back or they may think you have gone home.

Once your turn finally arrives, it is easy to forget all the questions you planned to ask. Many parents, including us, write them down beforehand as a reminder. Remember it is possible to phone afterwards to check on something you forgot about. No one is so important that you cannot contact them.

And finally

All the professionals working with your child are part of a team to which each contributes knowledge of his or her own special field. It is important to remember that you are part of that team too. Your speciality is your child. You are with him all the time and know him far better than anyone else. The professionals advise you how to care for your child. You decide how much of that advice to follow. You are best placed to see when different suggestions conflict with each other and to realize when you need extra help. Be confident – you are important too.

4

Doctors

When I talk to other parents about their contact with the various professionals, it is nearly always doctors who are mentioned first. This is hardly surprising as they give us the initial diagnosis, check our children's progress and link us with many of the other professions. For some of us, our dependence on doctors is enormous because our children depend on constant medical care for their quality and length of life.

Although the idea of doctors being second-only-to-God in importance has gone, many parents feel less at ease with them than with any of the other professionals they meet. I know I was more apprehensive about asking them to help with this book than I was of contacting anyone else. I need not have worried for, when I eventually plucked up my courage, they were very encouraging and helpful.

We expect high standards from doctors, higher perhaps than we would set for anyone else. We want them always to be available but never to make mistakes, even at two o'clock in the morning after a full day's work! We want them to really care about our child but never to let that caring cloud their medical judgement. We want them to allow us to stay with our children during treatment but not to let our nervous jitters make it harder for them to put a needle in a vein.

The ideal doctor, from a parent's viewpoint, shows that she cares about the whole family as well as having all the necessary medical skills. Not everyone finds this easy to do. Some offhand or distant behaviour by doctors is not callousness but shyness or a coping mechanism to enable them to work constantly with severely ill or handicapped children without cracking under the strain.

Family doctors

A good, understanding GP can make life much easier for you. As well as providing good care for your child, she will understand the stress you are under and be sympathetic if you develop health problems as a result.

Your GP can link you with much of the help available for your child, so she is a good person to talk to if you feel you are not receiving as much help as you need. She can refer you to a social worker, occupational therapist, speech therapist, dietician, physiotherapist or district nurse, as well as to specialist doctors.

Many parents go through agonies worrying when to phone the doctor. The golden rule is 'If in doubt, ask'. Find out from your GP and consultant if there are any special problems you should watch out for, or any conditions which need treating faster in your child than in a normal one. Ask them when to go to your GP and when to go directly to the hospital.

If your child develops symptoms which worry you, take him to the doctor or phone for advice. Don't worry about wasting your doctor's time. It is quite reasonable for you to need help to learn to distinguish between what matters and what doesn't.

Your GP is only human and will prefer her spare time to remain uninterrupted and to have an unbroken night's sleep. Don't phone out-of-hours about something which could reasonably wait until tomorrow. If your child is off-colour and likely to deteriorate to the point of needing a doctor by the evening, contact your doctor *before* she goes home rather than hanging on until she is in the middle of her tea. Similarly, it is preferable to phone early in the evening than delay and end up dragging her out of bed in the small hours.

Don't allow the previous paragraph to stop you calling a doctor out-of-hours if you really need one. No good doctor minds being called out if there is a genuine need. Neither will she mind you phoning for advice if you are genuinely worried and don't know whether you need her or not.

Sometimes the GP you contact will not be your own, perhaps because your doctor shares 'on call' with colleagues or because you (or she) are on holiday. It is important to make sure the new doctor has all the relevant information: child's age, handicap (if relevant), any current treatment (especially names of drugs) as well as the current symptoms. Make sure she knows if your child is particularly at risk, perhaps because he is very chesty, has a weak heart or is liable to fits with a high temperature.

A strange GP is likely to know less than you about your child's condition, especially if it is rare. Although she may resent you telling her what to do, comments like 'My doctor usually gives him Septrin' may be welcome. If she is really in doubt, you could suggest she phones the hospital for advice. Some parents find it helps to plan ahead for this problem occurring on holiday by taking a letter from their doctor or hospital recommending any medical treatment which may be necessary.

Hospital doctors

So far I have talked about consultants when referring to hospital doctors. They are the most senior doctors in a hospital and the ones you are most likely to see at outpatient clinics. They make decisions on treatment without reference to anyone else and leave the routine work, like chasing X-rays, to the more junior members of staff. They are also involved in teaching, hospital organization and management.

At the next level down are the senior registrar (SR) and registrar, although the SR may be missing from smaller hospitals. They are both experienced doctors who make decisions themselves and order treatments, although they work under the guidance of a consultant. Even if your child is officially under a consultant, you may see a registrar or senior registrar most of the time, especially if she has a particular interest in your child's condition.

The most junior level in a speciality like paediatrics is the senior house officer (SHO). As she is young and probably the first doctor you meet on admission, she may seem the most approachable. However, she will only have qualified a year or two ago so may not be the best person to answer complicated questions about your child's condition or treatment.

Communications

When your GP first asks a consultant to see your child, she will write a referral letter outlining the problem. After your first hospital visit, the consultant will write to your GP saying what she has found and what action is necessary. This letter may not arrive for a couple of weeks because of delays in typing so don't assume your GP will immediately know what the hospital have said. If urgent communication is necessary, the consultant may phone your GP or send a handwritten or verbal message with you.

Ideally, she will also write to your GP after each subsequent visit but this is not always possible in very busy clinics, like the fracture clinic. Then the consultant will only write if there is anything significant to report, such as a change in condition or treatment.

If your child needs surgery or treatment in hospital the consultant

26

will arrange this. If continuing medical treatment at home is needed, she will advise your GP what to do. Note the word 'advise'. Technically, GPs are in charge of their patients' care; consultants can only suggest treatments, not order them.

Some GPs welcome the consultant's advice, working as a team with the hospital in caring for your child or even allowing the hospital total control. Others only accept the advice grudgingly while some really resent it, taking the attitude 'He's my patient and I'll do what I think'.

Occasionally, a GP refuses to prescribe a drug recommended by the hospital. If this happens to you, ask your GP to explain her reasons and to reconsider her decision. If that gets you nowhere, contact the consultant and ask her to help by talking to your GP. If neither of these approaches work, the only solution is to change your doctor.

Your GP is unlikely to keep the hospital informed about treatments she gives so you will have to update your consultant at outpatient clinics. If your memory is anywhere near as bad as mine, it is worth noting down which antibiotics and other drugs your child is prescribed and what they were for. Otherwise the simple question 'How's he been keeping?' can throw you into confusion.

Communication problems can also occur if your child is being treated by more than one consultant. In theory, your GP co-ordinates the various treatments. If she doesn't (which is quite likely), it is usually the paediatrician at the hospital who is the best one to be in control. She is more accustomed to considering the whole child than a doctor specializing in another field of medicine and is also more likely to be a good communicator. If you are confused by a battery of consultants and no one seems to be co-ordinating their work, ask the most sympathetic one for help.

Specialists

There is an increasing tendency for consultants and hospitals to develop special interests which results in some units having particular expertise in individual fields of childhood illness. If such a unit exists for your child's condition, it is usually worth taking your child there even if it is some distance away. The unit should be able to give the best possible treatment as it will have more experience of his condition and the most up-to-date information available on current research. Not only will the doctor be more aware of your

27

child's needs, but the other staff like physiotherapists and nurses will be too. The rarer your child's condition the more this advice applies.

Unless you are fortunate enough to have a specialist unit locally, you will end up with your child being treated by a GP, a local hospital and the specialist hospital. This can cause communication problems, especially if your local consultant resents the advice from the specialist because she is unwilling to admit another consultant knows more than her. This professional pride may also account for the difficulty some parents have experienced in persuading their local consultant to refer them to a specialist. If you meet this problem, ask your GP to refer you instead.

If you have a good GP and your specialist hospital is reasonably easy to reach, you may decide to omit visits to the local hospital as it has little to offer on a routine basis. However, if you live a great distance from the specialist, a system of shared care between the two hospitals may be more appropriate. For example, some cystic fibrosis (CF) children attend a regional CF clinic for an annual check but receive the rest of their care from their local hospitals.

Changing doctors

There are two main reasons why you might consider changing doctors. First, you may have lost confidence in your existing one. Maybe she failed to diagnose your child's condition for months or she refuses to follow the hospital's advice. Whatever the reason, you no longer have faith in her abilities. Second, even when you like your existing doctor, you may know of someone else who would be better because she has more interest in and experience with children like yours.

Perhaps you are hesitant to change doctors for fear of hurting people's feelings. I know we were before we did it. All the doctors I have spoken to were adamant that you should not compromise in trying to get the best care possible for your child just because you are worried about upsetting people. As a consultant paediatrician put it: 'You owe no loyalty to your GP or your consultant. Your loyalty is owed to your child.'

No one can please all the people all of the time so every doctor will find some patients who lose confidence in her and wish to change. Although all doctors lose some patients, most also gain some from other doctors.

Your doctor will probably feel upset if you change but her upset will be directed more at her failure with you than at your actions. Of course, if you have really become at loggerheads with her, she may be as pleased to see you leave as you are to go.

Don't commit yourself to leaving until you are sure there is somewhere better to go. Asking other parents can give you a good indication of the most sympathetic local doctors. If you want to change consultants but are too shy to tell your existing one, ask your GP to refer you to someone else. He may suggest an alternative if you cannot.

If you are planning to change GP, make an appointment to visit the one you would prefer. That gives you a chance to check you like her and to find out if she is willing to have your family on her list. If your chosen doctor is in the same group practice as your existing one, she may not feel it is diplomatic for you to change officially. However, she may be willing to see your child all the time anyway.

5

Health Visitors and Community Nurses

Health visitors

A health visitor is a qualified nurse with at least three months midwifery experience who has completed a special training course. Although the course lasts a year and is very intensive, it has to cover a wide range of subjects so your health visitor may have only limited experience in the needs of special children and their families. However, she should know where to look for more information to fill the gaps in her knowledge. Her main concern is with pre-school children and their families and you are automatically referred to her when your baby is born.

Personality matters

The amount of support you receive from your health visitor is very dependent on her personality, her interest in children like yours and whether you actually like each other. Many Mums find their health visitor invaluable. One even described hers as 'like a second Mum'. However not everyone is as fortunate.

If you find yours less than helpful, it could just be because she does not understand your needs. If you ask her for specific information, she may be more useful. You can also try telling her how you feel and pointing out as calmly as possible anything she does which upsets you (like expecting you to attend the baby clinic, for example). Once she understands your feelings, her attitude may improve.

Ask if there is a health visitor for special-needs children in your area. If there is, ask to be referred to her as she should have more information and a much greater understanding of how you feel. She should also have contacts with the local support services.

If your child's problems were not diagnosed or did not develop until after he started school, you will probably have lost contact with your health visitor. If you liked her, there is nothing to stop you contacting her again for information and advice on local support services. It is also still worth asking about a specialist health visitor as she may, like our local one, deal with special-needs children of all ages.

Available help

Your health visitor is a good source of information and advice. As well as ordinary information about child care, she can advise you on nursing techniques which might be useful, although she will not carry them out for you. She should know about the help available locally and she can contact other agencies like the social services on your behalf. She may also be willing to contact charities for you to arrange funding for any extra help or equipment you need. This is particularly useful if (like me) you find it difficult to ask for help yourself.

If your child is incontinent, your health visitor may be able to provide incontinence aids such as disposable nappies and plastic pants. Several mothers have complained to me that they only learnt about this service by chance so it is worth asking if it exists.

Community nurses

Whereas all families with young children will have a health visitor automatically, you will usually only have visits from a community (or district) nurse if your child has been referred to her by your GP or hospital. If you think a community nurse could help you, ask your GP to arrange it.

Although a doctor asks her to visit you originally, it is your nurse who decides what care to offer and how long and how frequently to continue visiting. Like a health visitor, she can contact other people on your behalf such as social services or the housing department. She can suggest items which would simplify your child's care and advise you on how to get them. In particular, she may liase with your local Red Cross Society to borrow equipment and she may be able to supply disposable nappies if your child is incontinent.

Unlike a health visitor, your community nurse can offer practical nursing help. She can perform skilled tasks such as changing dressings and giving injections. She can also teach you any nursing techniques you need such as preventing bedsores.

Even if you do not need her help all the time, she may prove invaluable should your child's needs increase temporarily, perhaps after an operation. She is also a source of possible help if you are temporarily incapacitated and need help with giving your child nursing care. For example, she may be able to assist with bathing your immobile child if you break your arm or hurt your back.

31

6

Social Workers

Whereas all families with young children have a health visitor, they don't all have a social worker. However, many parents of sick or handicapped children do have social work support to help them meet the extra demands they face. Most social workers are employed by local authority social services departments and are based either in local social services offices or in hospitals. The rest are employed by the larger voluntary societies.

How to get a social worker

You can be referred to a social worker by your health visitor, doctor, teacher or by yourself. Many people refer themselves so no one will be surprised if you do. Phone or visit your local social services office or hospital social worker. If you contact social services, you will talk to the duty officer who will try to organize immediate attention if you need it urgently. More usually, she will pass your enquiry to a senior social worker who will decide who should follow it up. Don't be surprised if the person who deals with you eventually is not the one you first spoke to. It is just the way the system works, and not, as one mother felt, a sign your case has been kicked around the office.

Some social services departments are organized generically which means all the social workers do a bit of everything. Others are divided into departments for mental handicap, child care, mental illness etc. Don't assume you automatically need a child care social worker. Sometimes someone from the mental handicap or elderly and physically handicapped teams would be more useful. There may also be someone specializing in helping the visually handicapped or hearing-impaired.

A medical social worker based at your hospital may be able to offer you good support, especially if she has experience with other children like yours. If the hospital is some way from your home, she may have only limited knowledge of the help you could receive locally but she should be able to suggest other people you could contact. If she works at a small, local hospital, she may have less experience of your specific situation but more knowledge of local services.

Getting along

Social work training covers many areas so only a limited amount of time can be devoted to the needs of handicapped and sick children and their families. If you are lucky, your social worker will have specialized in this area after qualifying so she will know the problems you face and have sensible ideas on how to cope with them. However, if she has no experience with families like yours, she may have only limited understanding of your needs. If she misunderstands your situation and offers inappropriate help, tell her so as calmly as you can. Try stating your needs very specifically: ask for the exact help or information you need.

Personality probably matters more with social workers than with any of the other professionals. How can you be expected to talk about your deepest concerns to someone you don't like? If you find it difficult to get on with your social worker, talk to her team leader or senior – ask the secretaries at her office to put you in touch. Be diplomatic. There's no need to call your social worker 'an insensitive cow', just say you find it difficult to confide in her. The senior will understand your need to relate to someone and should either arrange for a change of social worker or try to persuade the existing one to improve.

What help is available?

Contrary to popular opinion social workers don't delight in taking children away from their parents. Your social worker would rather help you to cope than end up with your child in care. If she offers you *respite* care of some sort (see Chapter 16), this is not the thin end of the wedge. She is trying to give you a breathing space, not stealing your child away.

As well as respite care, your social worker may be able to organize help with alterations to your home, special equipment, home helps and home sitters, although resources vary widely from area to area and their availability is limited by cost. Some social services departments also use 'approved' volunteers to provide a wide range of help.

Your social worker should know about local facilities like toy libraries and opportunity playgroups and can also explain the various benefits to which you may be entitled and help you complete the application forms. In addition, she may know of charities which could help and be willing to contact them for you.

7

Therapists

Physiotherapists, occupational therapists and speech therapists all work with sick and handicapped children to help them overcome their difficulties. If you feel your child would benefit from such help, ask for it as soon as you can for the earlier treatment starts the better.

Physiotherapists

'Physios' are probably the best known of the therapists who work with children with special needs. They use exercises to help their patients gain and keep the best possible use of their bodies. They also try to improve breathing, to prevent the development of deformities and to slow down the deterioration caused by some progressive diseases.

Physios usually work in hospitals although some are attached to special schools and clinics. If you think physiotherapy could help your child, ask your doctor to refer you. You will probably have to take your child to see her although some physios visit children at home.

It is worth asking to see a children's physio if there is one available. Not only is it more likely that she will have had experience of your child's condition but she will also be used to working with uncooperative young patients.

The physio will assess your child's problems and teach you exercises to do with him at home. She may also show you ways to handle your child which will encourage good patterns of movement. If he needs lifting a good deal, ask her to show you how to do this without straining your back. That advice comes from the heart as I hurt my back lifting a profoundly handicapped girl we know. The result was extremely painful and meant I could not carry her or anything else for several months.

If your child receives physio at school, try to learn the exercises so you can continue with them during the holidays. Otherwise he may lose some of his hard won progress which will be very disappointing for everyone, especially him.

There are a variety of ideas among physios about the best way to treat some conditions, especially cerebral palsy. If you believe a different approach would be better for your child, ask your doctor to refer you to a clinic which uses it. Judging by the experience of other parents, you may need to be persistent in your request as doctors and physios are understandably resistant to suggestions that someone else can do better than they can.

Occupational therapy

Occupational therapists (OTs) work with children to increase their ability to cope with the tasks presented by everyday life. Their work not only covers areas like dressing but also less obvious ones like writing skills and difficulties with perception.

They also advise on special equipment to make life easier. In particular, they can assess for and provide wheelchairs and special seats, and advise you on how to position and handle your child. This may be important for your child as good handling techniques and seating can prevent or minimize future problems with some conditions, especially cerebral palsy.

In some ways the aims of occupational therapists overlap with those of physios as improving your child's ability to feed himself, for example, will probably involve improving his use of his arms and hands. OTs achieve their aims through games and activities rather than formal exercises but, to further fudge the difference, physios working with children often turn their exercises into games to make them more enjoyable.

If you have both a physio and an OT working with your child, they will usually talk together to ensure their treatments complement each other. It is very unlikely that they will give you conflicting advice, but if they do, point this out so they can sort the matter out between them.

OTs are either employed by a local authority, the NHS or by one of the voluntary societies. Local authority OTs are attached to the social services or education departments. They advise on the provision of special equipment and on necessary adaptations at home or in school. Time does not usually allow them to carry out treatment schemes with individual clients. Most of their work is with physically handicapped adults and the elderly but they also work with special-needs children and their families.

You can refer yourself to a local authority OT by contacting your local social services department. Ask if there is a paediatric OT as some councils employ one and she will have better knowledge of the equipment available for children.

An OT employed by the NHS is usually hospital-based, although that does not prevent her working with children in their own homes or at school. Ask your doctor to refer you if you think an OT could help. Once again, ask for a paediatric OT if possible.

Once you are referred, the OT will carry out a complete assessment of your child's abilities and problems. Usually a copy of the assessment is sent to your doctor and sometimes one is given to you as well. The OT then devises a programme of activities to develop his abilities to the full and to give him methods of coping with tasks which his disabilities prevent him doing normally. She does not carry out all the training herself. Instead she will teach you activities to do at home and she may encourage staff at his school to do them too.

Speech therapists

A speech therapist can work with any child with a communication problem even if this is linked to another disability like deafness or mental handicap. Because eating involves similar mouth and tongue control to speaking, a speech therapist can also help if your child has feeding difficulties.

Most speech therapists are employed by health authorities to work in hospitals, clinics, schools and in the community visiting patients at home. There are also some practising privately but treatment by one of them would involve you paying fees. You can be referred to a speech therapist by your GP, consultant, health visitor or school or you can contact one yourself if you prefer.

The main problem parents find with speech therapists is getting one at all. In some areas of the country, speech therapy is a scarce resource which cannot stretch to all the children needing it. The result is some children receiving no help and others receiving less than they need.

If you are concerned that your child does not see his speech therapist as often as you would like, talk about your worries at your next visit. You may be worrying unnecessarily, or his treatment could be limited by shortage of resources. Perhaps she could teach you ways to help him at home which would fill the gaps between lessons.

8

Psychiatrists, Psychologists and Psychotherapists

I am sure I am not alone in finding this group of professionals particularly confusing. Both their names and their roles seem so similar that it is hard for outsiders like us to understand the difference between them.

Educational psychologists are employed by local education authorities and work mainly in schools (see Chapter 9). Clinical psychologists work with psychiatrists and psychotherapists in teams based in family therapy (or child guidance) units or hospitals. Children referred to such a team receive help from whichever person seems most appropriate. The choice may be as dependent on individual personalities as on qualifications because there is some overlap between the three roles. In fact, some psychiatrists and psychologists are also trained psychotherapists.

A psychiatrist, clinical psychologist or psychotherapist is most likely to be useful if your child has difficult behaviour, problems caused by stress or a mental handicap. Referral is usually through your GP but could be through your hospital doctor.

Psychiatrists

Child psychiatrists are doctors who have specialized in emotional and behavioural problems and mental illness and then taken additional post-qualification training in child psychiatry. Because they are medically qualified, they can prescribe drugs but that does not mean they automatically do so. They also use other treatments like counselling and psychotherapy.

Clinical psychologists

Clinical psychologists have a qualification in psychology which means they have studied human behaviour and how we think and learn. They apply this knowledge to help people with behavioural problems or emotional difficulties like anxiety and depression. They can use a variety of tests to find out about your child's intelligence, interests and personality. They can also teach you behaviour modification techniques to try to change and improve your child's behaviour. These are similar to methods used by many parents and can involve rewards for good behaviour or deterrents to bad behaviour (like temporary removal to a less interesting place). Psychologists may also use counselling and psychotherapy.

Psychotherapists

Child psychotherapists have undertaken several years study and training after obtaining a degree. They undergo personal psycho-therapy as part of their course which helps them understand themselves better as well as giving them an insight into how it feels to receive psychotherapy.

Child psychotherapists look for the reasons for a child's behaviour problems and try to help him understand and deal with stresses in his past or present life. For example, some psycho-therapists work with children who need help to face long-term illness or disability.

Psychotherapy works through long, regular sessions over a considerable period of time which enable the worker to gain your child's trust. He plays while the therapist only talks when it seems appropriate.

The toys and play materials are chosen by the therapist for their ability to be used to express feelings. They are more likely to include craft materials, cars and families of dolls than the latest highly advertised toys. Similar play therapy techniques may also be used sometimes by other professionals like social workers and trained counsellors.

Your involvement

Whichever type of person is working with your child, she will probably want to talk to you as well. You can help her understand your child's background. She may offer ideas to help your child at home and perhaps offer explanations of his behaviour which may make it easier for you to tolerate.

All these professionals are trained to be good listeners. You may find it disconcerting the first time you meet one if you are used to professionals who talk all the time and pay little heed to your opinions. The pauses they leave to allow you time to think and reply may feel, at first, like long embarrassing silences. In the long run, you may benefit both from having someone to talk to and from having a better understanding of your child.

9

Educational Specialists

Apart from schoolteachers, your education department employs several other people who can help your child. Those you are most likely to meet are the educational psychologist, the education welfare officer, the special-needs adviser and the home teacher.

Educational psychologists

Either you or the school may ask the educational psychologist to see your child. The school would probably prefer your request to be made through them but you are free to make contact yourself if the school is reluctant or uncooperative.

Your educational psychologist is a very knowledgeable person. As well as being a fully qualified psychologist, she is also a trained teacher with at least two years teaching experience, often with children with special needs. As a result, she should be able to assess your child's abilities and learning difficulties fully and see how his needs can be catered for best in the classroom. Some teachers are more willing to acknowledge a child has problems at school if an educational psychologist confirms that the difficulties really exist and suggests ways to overcome them.

Your educational psychologist should also have a good knowledge of the local schools and their abilities at coping with special-needs children. Although officially she may be forced to take the line that all the authority's schools are equally good, she may be able to give you detailed, informal advice and support your application for your child to attend a particular school.

You may find you do not agree with the educational psychologist's assessment of your child or the education authority's recommendations for his education. It is possible to ask for an independent educational psychologist to assess your child and to give you a second opinion. Your voluntary society may know of someone suitable or you can contact The Independent Panel of Special Education Experts for advice.

Education welfare officers

Years ago, the education welfare officer (EWO) was known as the truant officer. The job is now much wider, involving many aspects of social work, although it does still include checking up on children who are away from school.

The EWO acts as a link between school and home. In that role, she can be particularly useful if your child is away a great deal. You can contact her if you are finding difficulty obtaining work from school or feel your child needs home tuition. She is also another person who can ask social services to help your family.

There is probably an EWO allocated to your school: ask the school secretary who it is. If there is not one or she is unobtainable or ineffective, try contacting the Principal EWO whose office will be in the same place as the rest of the education department's central bureaucracy.

Your education welfare department organizes school transport for those children who need it as well as allocating help such as free school meals and uniform grants. Where I live, home tutors for sick children are organized through Education Welfare although this may be the job of the special-needs adviser in your area.

Special-needs adviser

Your local authority almost certainly has someone in this role although the title may be slightly different: Inspector of Special Needs Provision is one alternative. As the name suggests, she is employed by your education authority to advise the Chief Education Officer on the resources required by pupils with special needs and on any issues relevant to those children's education.

She can advise schools on the best way to react to and provide for the special needs of individual children. She also liaises with the parents of the children and with voluntary societies, the health authority and social services. You can contact her directly if you are concerned that your child is not receiving the special help you believe he needs and if talking to the school has not improved matters (either because of lack of co-operation or lack of resources).

Home teacher for pre-school children

Many education authorities now employ a home teacher to work with pre-school special-needs children. She visits the children regularly in their own homes, showing parents how to help their child to learn. Many home teachers use the Portage System of teaching which uses games and activities to help children learn the skills they need. Some teachers use the system exclusively while others incorporate it with other approaches.

Most parents speak highly of their home teacher, finding that her visits break their isolation as well as helping their child. One mum even said that, if she had to choose only one professional to help her, it would be the home teacher. It is a job which seems to attract warm, friendly people who really care about the children they visit.

To find out if a home teacher exists in your area, ask your local education department. They should also be able to explain the system for referral which varies from area to area.

10
Standing up for your Child

Sadly, at some stage you may feel your child is not receiving the best possible help. Perhaps essential equipment has still not arrived, months after it was requested, the DSS has refused Attendance Allowance when you are sure you are entitled to it or your education authority is refusing to send your child to the school best suited to his needs because it is outside their area. Whatever the problem, you can help your child by standing up for his rights. Don't assume no one will take any notice. People will read your letters and listen to what you say.

Find out what the problem is

Before you can decide what action to take, you need to know why the problem has arisen. Is the education authority refusing to send your child to the school because of cost or because it is full? Did the DSS base their decision on the correct facts or did the visiting doctor complete the form incorrectly? Has your occupational therapist forgotten to order the equipment or is she doing her best but being thwarted by manufacturer's delays?

Suppose, for example, you are angry because your child had to wait three hours before a doctor set up an intravenous drip. This may have been unavoidable because all the available doctors were busy saving another child's life. Alternatively, a junior doctor may have dozed off over his coffee after working 48 hours without sleep or the doctor concerned may have been lazy and inefficient. Only in the last case, might a complaint about the doctor be justified. In the first case it would be unreasonable while in the second you might consider complaining instead about the system which made the doctor so tired in the first place. You will only know which action to take when you understand the background to the situation.

To find out the reasons for your problem, contact the person or people concerned or their immediate superior. Your consultant is a good person to contact about difficulties arising in hospital. Describe the situation worrying you and ask why it happened. It can help the person to reply if you ask specific questions rather than just asking for a general explanation. For instance, you could ask the DSS for a copy of the visiting doctor's report.

Once you know what is wrong, you need to decide what action to take (if any). Be reasonable! No system is perfect and everyone makes mistakes sometimes. Your complaint will be taken more seriously if you are usually reasonable and friendly than if you are constantly grumbling about every little thing.

A letter or a phone call?

A phone call has the advantage of being quick but it is easily forgotten, misheard or misunderstood. It also requires an immediate response which is often not as good as one given after more thought. A written complaint or enquiry is better as it provides a permanent account of the problem for reference and allows time for a well-considered reply.

When writing, keep to the point and be clear and specific. If you are complaining that your child was given the wrong dose of a drug, don't fudge the issue by adding grumbles about the sogginess of the hospital chips. If you are writing about a particular incident give the date it occurred and, if possible, name the people involved.

It is better to send your letter to an individual rather than a department as personally addressed mail is often dealt with first. It is worth phoning before you write just to find the name of the correct person. If you are in doubt over who to contact, aim high. Send your letter to the head of the organization or department. He or she will pass your letter down to the correct person where it will probably be dealt with before a similar one passed up from someone lower down. Never think someone is too important for you to contact.

Finding help and information

It is much easier to deal with bureaucracy if you know your rights and how the system works. Your voluntary society may be able to help as well as the other organizations which offer help and advice to ordinary people dealing with authority.

Your local Citizens Advice Bureau is a good source of up-to-date information on many issues and may be particularly knowledgeable about your local situation. They can help you understand the information and advise you who to to contact. They can be particularly helpful with problems over benefits, an area where the Disability Alliance and social workers may also be useful.

DIAL is a nationwide network of advice centres run by and for disabled people. Your local group should be able to help you find and understand the information you need. They, like the CAB, will know your local situation and may well have useful contacts.

The Advisory Centre for Education runs a free helpline for parents on weekday afternoons which I have always found extremely useful. They also publish *The Ace Special Education Handbook* which gives clear explanations of the law about special education and advice for parents on handling a variety of situations. It even includes specimen letters as a guide for writing your own.

Your local Community Health Council provides an advisory service to the public on all aspects of health care. They can talk through your worries to help you decide if you have a genuine cause for complaint or have just misunderstood something. They cannot investigate your complaint but they can tell you who to contact and help you decide which points to make in your letter. If you find letter writing difficult, they may even write it for you. If you are dissatisfied with the answers you receive to your enquiries, they can explain what action you should take next.

If you feel legal advice is necessary, you could try a law centre (or similar organization) if there is one near you. Network for the Handicapped and the Children's Legal Centre also offer advice on legal issues and Action for Victims of Medical Accidents may be able to help if your problem fits their field of interest. If you want to consult a solicitor, find one who is experienced with your type of problem as solicitors specialize in various aspects of the law. Also ask about charges and whether you are entitled to legal aid as lawyers' fees can easily mount to very high levels.

Be assertive not aggressive

'Don't be aggressive' is much easier advice to give than to follow. I have lost my temper a few times with officials but I have always regretted it. Once you have lost your temper, you have lost control of yourself and the situation. If you shout at someone, they are likely to lose any sympathy they may have felt for you. You put them on the defensive when they may have been helpful.

Unless the matter is so urgent that it can't wait, never complain when you are angry. Wait until you have calmed down, before you take any action. What you say and write then is likely to be far better thought out and more effective. It is better to sound determined than cross.

Actions like taking notes at a meeting and asking the name of the person to whom you are speaking can show you mean business. Also both Mum and Dad attending meetings can demonstrate the depth of your concern. Some bureaucrats still take complaints more seriously if they come from Dad rather than Mum.

Keep records

When dealing with officialdom, keep records so you can refer back to them if necessary. You don't need a complicated system – a large envelope or carrier bag will do. Keep all the letters you receive with a note of when they arrived. Also keep copies (however rough) of all the letters you send and date them. Write down the date of each relevant phone call you make or receive, together with a note of the name of the person you spoke to and what was said. If you need to refer to a phone call, it sounds better if you can say who you spoke to. Also, officials are less likely to make glib promises they do not intend to keep if they know the statements can be traced back to them.

Don't be unnecessarily hurtful

In Eastern countries, people believe it is important not to lose face. The same principle applies here: no one likes being made to look foolish, lazy or incompetent. If you back someone into a psychological corner so he cannot satisfy your demands without losing face, he may resist you even more stubbornly than before. It is sometimes worth compromising on unimportant side-issues so the bureaucrats can be left feeling they did not give way completely.

Don't be unnecessarily hurtful. Give praise for the good things as well as criticism of the bad. It costs nothing and gives you a better chance of a reasonable working relationship with officialdom after this particular issue is settled. There is nothing to be gained from being permanently at loggerheads with everyone.

Counting the cost can help

Bureaucrats push pieces of paper around. They have little contact with the people they affect by their decisions. Consequently, an argument based on financial reasons can sometimes do better than one based purely on humanitarian ones.

Suppose, for example, that you are to have an operation and have asked for help with caring for your severely handicapped child at home while your husband is at work. The authorities say this is not possible but have offered to place your child in a residential home until you are well again.

If you try to persuade the bureaucrats that their idea will have a bad emotional effect on your child and the rest of the family, you may well get nowhere. However, a carefully thought out argument comparing the costs of the two solutions could be very effective.

Make a fuss

Suppose you have tried as hard as you can to persuade the authorities to provide the help you believe your child needs but to no avail. Perhaps you have tried all available appeals procedures without success. Perhaps the authorities are just producing endless delays and incomprehensible replies full of legalistic jargon. Perhaps you are not even getting replies at all. What can you do now?

The answer is to make a fuss. Start by contacting your local councillor if your local authority is the problem. If that has no effect or is inapplicable, write to your MP. It is amazing how a letter from the House of Commons can speed up the tardiest of officials and produce long, polite letters of explanation where previously you only received curt notes of indecipherable jargon. One bureaucrat likened the effect of an MP's letter arriving in the office to that of a bomb exploding. He added one note of caution though. The effect diminishes with repetition so don't involve your MP too soon. Save his support until you really need it.

Before I started this chapter I contacted Jack Ashley MP, who has campaigned on behalf of the disabled for many years. With his kind permission, I quote the following advice from his reply:

I would emphasise to the parents that it is very important not to be put off by bureaucracy, nor to be deterred by difficulties. It is very important to be persistent and for them to insist on action. If they happen to find they are getting nowhere, then I strongly advise them to contact press, radio and television because publicity is a formidable weapon and parents who have been neglected or deprived of their rights should have no hesitation in using it if necessary.

This is good advice based on years of experience, so use it. Sometimes just mentioning you are considering contacting the media can have the desired effect. People don't like being on the receiving end of bad publicity especially if they are hoping for promotion or re-election. Publicity may also help you contact other parents fighting the same battles so you can unite and campaign together.

Many of the national and local papers like campaigning for better treatment of the more vulnerable members of society. A special-needs child who is being refused necessary help makes a good story so it is often easy to obtain the publicity you need. Television and radio will sometimes take up such an item too, either following up a press story or providing the initial publicity in campaigning programmes like 'That's Life' or 'Watchdog'.

Parents do have power

You are not powerless. You can influence events. Much of the help available now for sick and handicapped children started as a result of pressure from parents. Some schemes were started by the parents themselves.

Remember, the walls of Jericho fell down when all the trumpets sounded at once, not one at a time. If the problem you face affects many parents, get together to campaign for better help: there is power in numbers.

PART THREE
Coping

11
Facing the Outside World

First reactions

When a new baby is born, there are socially accepted responses for friends and relatives to make. They ask how much it weighs, what sex it is and all the other conventional questions. When a child is born with problems or develops them later, social custom offers no guidelines so no one is quite sure what to do or say.

Some people will cope with the situation and show by their words or actions that they care about you and your child. Others will try to find the right words but fail, not because they care any less but because they are less able to judge your needs. Their words may not only fail to comfort you but can make you feel even worse. Comments like 'Look on the bright side – things could be worse' are well-intentioned but may feel more hurtful than helpful. Try not to condemn people forever because of their early inability to understand how you feel; they were probably doing their best.

Some of your friends may need time to accept your new situation before they feel able to talk to you. Most will eventually overcome their nervousness but some may never be able to adapt to what has happened. Let them go and try not to be too hurt by their behaviour. In time, new friends will take their place.

If your child's problems are not visible, other people may not understand fully the impact the diagnosis has had on you. This can lead them to make unintentionally hurtful comments. Remember they are not being deliberately unpleasant and may not even realize they have upset you. If a friend or relative is particularly thoughtless, it may be best to avoid him or her for a while until you are feeling less vulnerable.

Talking to people

At first, people outside your immediate circle may feel awkward when they meet you. The local grapevine will have told them something is wrong but, if it is anything like our local one, their knowledge will be vague, patchy or inaccurate and they won't know what to say. You will probably feel equally awkward as you will not

51

know how much information they have already heard. The simple question 'How's the baby?' used to throw me in confusion when Matthew was first born. I never knew if the questioner was just asking out of social convention or was genuinely concerned because she knew he had cystic fibrosis.

If you would rather not discuss your child's condition with all and sundry, keep the conversation on safer topics. However, if you are happy talking about your child's problems, you can bring up the subject yourself. Use the words you feel comfortable with and prefer: e.g. Down's Syndrome rather than 'mongol', cerebral palsy rather than 'spastic'. Most people will follow your lead. Some parents find it best to mention their children's problems early in a new friendship as the longer they delay, the more embarrassed the other person may be when they do find out.

If people start talking about your child as if he is not there, bring him into the conversation yourself. In particular, if your child is very severely handicapped, some thoughtless people may make comments in front of him like 'Children like that should be allowed to die'. It is important, for your child's sake, that you not only disagree but point out that he may well understand everything he hears.

Too much help?

Some people are so anxious to help that they try to give assistance when you don't want it. This is particularly likely when your child is struggling to do something by himself. Strangers may be so upset by his slow progress that they step in and do it themselves. This can be annoying and frustrating so try to spot trouble coming. If you see someone about to help unnecessarily, stop them and explain why it is better for your child to manage on his own.

Please try to be as pleasant as you can, although I know it can be difficult at times. If you are rude, that person may hesitate to help someone else who really needs it. Remember, too, that you are providing a model for your child to follow as he gets older. Although now it is right for him to struggle on his own, he may find eventually that he has to accept occasional help if he is going to cope alone.

Rude comments

It always amazes me how much some total strangers will interfere.

Comments like 'He needs a good hiding' or 'You should take him to a doctor with a cough like that' are not at all uncommon. One way to react is to ignore the speaker, especially if you are never likely to see them again. Alternatively, you say 'It's none of your business' or some other rude retort. Although that can be effective, it can leave you tense and bad-tempered.

A third option is to provide a brief explanation which stops the comments without you losing your temper. This is particularly worthwhile with strangers who you are likely to meet again (local shop assistants, for example) as it stops the situation recurring. You don't need to relate your child's entire medical history. Just use a simple explanation which you feel comfortable giving – perhaps that your child is deaf, can't see well or finds it hard to learn.

Staring

Staring is a common problem for parents whose children are noticeably handicapped. In fact, it bothers anyone who looks different, whether they are handicapped or not – mothers of identical twins complain about it too. Not everyone who stares at your child is thinking unpleasant things about him or extreme pity for you. Many are just interested or curious. There is no way to stop it completely, so try to grow a thicker skin.

If the situation is too bad to tolerate, try staring back – it works sometimes. Another method is to talk to the people who are staring, explaining your child's condition. Once their curiosity is satisfied, they will probably lose interest.

Don't hide at home

Don't let the responses of local people stop you taking your child out and about. Staring and rude comments are a reaction to seeing something different – your child. The more they see him, the sooner he will cease to be unusual. As everyone becomes accustomed to him, the stares and the comments will become less common. If you go out regularly, both you and your child will benefit from seeing different people and places.

12

Finding the Time
and the Money

Caring for any child takes huge amounts of time, energy and
money. Your child's special needs will make even greater demands
on you in all three areas. No amount of wishing can make you grow
an extra pair of hands or add an extra hour to the day. Instead you
need to use all the help available and look for ways to cut your
workload.

Lighten the housework load

Housework is a strange commodity. It expands to fit the time
available so if you have all day, that's how long it takes. However, if
someone phones to say they will be visiting you in half an hour, it is
amazing how you can turn chaos into order before they arrive.

It follows that one way to speed up housework is to strictly limit
the time available. If you only have an hour to clean the house you
will either work faster or clean less thoroughly. Either way, at the
end of the time the job will be done. Try giving yourself an incentive
to finish by a set time: watching a TV programme, a walk in the park
or whatever works for you. If you choose something the children
will enjoy too, you may end up with some willing helpers.

Remember your home does not have to be spotless all the time –
that's an impossible target with children around. Accept that you
will be doing well if you keep your home reasonably clean and tidy.
When you decide which housework to let slide, choose the items
which matter least to everyone in the family. Personally I am ratty
and bad-tempered when the floors are dirty but I can ignore dirty
windows until I can barely see through them. For your family the
priorities will be different.

Do everything the easy way

Modern technology has created a host of appliances to ease the
workload at home. A good washing machine and tumble drier are
marvellous for any mum but particularly valuable if your child is

incontinent or vomits frequently. A freezer allows you to shop less often while a dishwasher frees time for other tasks.

All these gadgets are expensive but they are worth the money if you can stretch your budget enough to afford them. If not, help may be available from the Family Fund or charities. Ask your health visitor, social worker or voluntary society for ideas.

Look for easy ways of doing everything, especially the jobs you dislike. Choose clothes in easy-care fabrics and only iron the items which really need it. Only prepare elaborate meals if you love cooking; quick, simple food can be just as nutritious. If you hate shopping, try using a mail order catalogue.

Leave time for you

When you are deciding how to save time, don't make the mistake of ignoring your own needs. Skipping meals or eating on the run will leave you less physically able to cope. Time spent watching TV or reading is not wasted if it helps you relax. All work and no play makes you very tired and tired people make poorer use of their available time.

Combine activities

Although you have only one pair of hands, it is sometimes possible to do two things at once. Could some of your child's special help be combined with ordinary tasks? For example, can he practise his colours by matching the socks, or could you do some physio while he is playing in the bath?

Learn to say 'no'

'Can you run a stall at the school fête?' 'Please help with our flag day.' 'You will come to the prayer group, won't you?' The possible demands on your time from outside the family are endless. Learn to say 'No' to all of them except those you feel you will enjoy and which fit easily with the rest of your tasks.

You may feel particularly guilty not helping the voluntary society concerned with your child's problem. Some parents find it helps them to pour energy into fund-raising but many do not. They find such activities a great emotional strain especially if they have to keep justifying the society's aims to outsiders.

Don't let yourself be pushed into activites which make you feel uncomfortable. If you want to help but, like me, you can't face rattling collecting tins, perhaps you could do something else instead. How about addressing envelopes, talking to parents of newly diagnosed children or allowing your front room to be used for a parent's support group?

Many Christian parents find that a strong faith, prayer and the support of a loving church helps them cope better than they would have ever thought possible. However, church can be another pressure on your time which is hard to refuse. You may be asked to go to Bible class, help organize the parish supper or teach in Sunday School. Some people may even increase the pressure by insisting this is God's will or suggesting you are not a good Christian if you refuse.

If you are in this situation, don't allow yourself to be browbeaten. Looking after your family is a big job and you should not underestimate its importance. Pray about your problem and follow God's guidance, not other people's. Perhaps your role at the moment is to offer prayer support to those more actively involved in the church and to demonstrate Christian love and caring to the other people you meet in your daily life.

Claiming benefits

I am sure you already receive one Government allowance for your child – Child Benefit. It probably never occurred to you not to claim as you know you are entitled to it. You are equally entitled to any of the other benefits for which you qualify so don't feel guilty about claiming them either or let your pride prevent you accepting all the help available.

I am not describing the benefits available in detail as that information would soon become out of date. It is also too complicated a subject to describe accurately in the space I have available. *The Disability Rights Handbook* is an excellent guide with all the information you need on benefits. If you don't want to buy a copy yourself, your local CAB or DIAL group probably has one you can look at.

The two benefits designed for people with special needs are the Attendance Allowance and Mobility Allowance. It is often difficult to tell if your child is eligible for either of these benefits, particularly for attendance allowance, as the regulations are complicated to understand. If you are not sure, apply anyway. The worst that can happen is being turned down. Even then you can ask for your case to be reconsidered if you disagree with the decision as many such reviews are successful.

The Family Fund is different from other official help as, although it is funded by the government, it is run by the Joseph Rowntree Memorial Trust. If your child is severely handicapped, it may be able to give you grants for specific items you need to help you cope better. Parents who have used the Fund speak highly of the help available which is flexible enough to provide a wide range of items including household equipment, holidays and driving lessons. You ask for whatever you most need.

Help from charities

All over the country people are raising money to help others. Such fund-raising groups are often happy to provide special equipment for children like yours. Some will pay for other help like washing machines, hospital travelling expenses or holidays. The professionals working with you should know of charities willing to help and will often contact them on your behalf.

Perhaps you are unwilling to accept help from a charity; many people are. Charity has become something to be avoided at all costs. That is a pity as the original meaning of the word 'charity' is 'love'. If other people feel sufficient love for their fellow humans that they want to help you and your child, why not let them? Don't feel beholden. Take the gift of love in the spirit in which it is given and pass it on by showing love to others when you have the opportunity.

Some charities like to have a small presentation ceremony when equipment is handed over. They feel it helps their fund-raising by showing the money raised is put to good use. If you feel too shy or embarrassed to co-operate with such publicity, make sure the charity knows that early on. It can save disappointment and embarrassment later on. If your child is able to understand, ask his opinion too. He might have strong opinions for or against having his picture in the paper which don't match your own.

13

Making Life Easier

Special equipment can take many forms ranging from simple drinking cups to highly complex electronic communication aids and home extensions. Which items might help your child will depend on his particular problems.

Finding advice

It is very important to ask for advice before you get a specialized piece of equipment. Not only might the wrong item turn into a costly white elephant gathering dust in the corner, but it may actually impede your child's progress. The wrong gadget may give your child success at a task but stop him trying to do it properly. As a result, he may fail to develop new skills or lose old ones faster than his progressive disease dictates.

Probably the best person to ask is an occupational therapist. She is trained to assess your child's abilities and needs and will know many possible solutions to the problems you face. She will also have practical experience of many of the items under consideration and so be aware of additional snags or advantages which are not stated in the manufacturer's literature.

You may also gain ideas on equipment from your physiotherapist, health visitor, home teacher or other experts. If your child attends a special school, the staff may offer suggestions or he may use equipment there which you can see would be equally useful at home. Don't forget to consider your home situation as well. You don't want a hoist in the bathroom which prevents anyone getting to the toilet.

Special toys

Toy libraries provide an opportunity to try out a wide variety of toys and to borrow them for use at home. This is ideal as you then only buy toys which you know are suitable. Some toy libraries stock specially designed or adapted toys for handicapped children. Also Playmatters (previously called the Toy Library Association) can provide plans for making some special toys.

Your child's opinions are important

Even the most ideal equipment will be no good if your child refuses to use it. You will need to be particularly sensitive to his feelings if the new equipment is necessary because his condition has deteriorated. For example, if he is gradually losing the ability to walk he may be very resistant to accepting a wheelchair.

Involve him in the process of selection as much as possible so he does not feel the equipment is being foisted onto him. Try to be as positive as you can about the new item to encourage him to accept it. Hopefully any resistance he has will lessen once he realizes the equipment can make life better.

Meeting the cost

Special equipment is expensive. None of it sells in large enough quantities to benefit from the economy of mass production which keeps down the prices of televisions and washing machines. In fact, some of the items you need may have to be individually made for your child.

The NHS provides some equipment, like wheelchairs, which are needed for medical reasons. These items are provided free for children. Your local authority has a statutory obligation to supply aids to daily living such as gadgets to help with bathing and toiletting. Requests for these are made through an occupational therapist although your social worker, health visitor or community nurse may contact her for you.

Unfortunately, no amount of statutory obligation can enable your social services department to provide equipment when they have no money to pay for it. Economic restrictions on local government or a heavy demand for social services may result in severe limitations on your council's budget. You may be told that you will have to wait for the equipment you need until funds become available, perhaps until the new financial year, so try to plan ahead with your requests if you can. Sometimes making a fuss will push your equipment up the priority list (see Chapter 10).

Some equipment falls through the holes in the welfare net so no one is obliged to provide it. Physiotherapy equipment, like standing frames, rolls and wedges, fall into this category. Your OT, physio, social worker or health visitor can often arrange for you to get items that cannot be officially funded, perhaps by contacting charities on your behalf or arranging for you to borrow the equipment from somewhere. Your voluntary society may also be able to help.

Think ahead

Arranging finance takes time. Even when equipment is ordered, it may take a long time to come, especially if it needs to be specially made or adapted. It is therefore important to think ahead. Don't wait until your child is too heavy to lift before you ask for a hoist or you may end up struggling for ages.

Although your request for equipment may have been channelled through your OT, don't automatically assume that slow delivery is her fault. If you are angry about it, ask her the cause of the delay so your complaint can be directed at the right people.

Adapting and extending your home

Good housing makes life easier for everyone. It may be possible to alter your home to make life easier for you all. For example, if your child cannot walk, a downstairs bathroom or stairlift could save much lifting and wider doorways could make the whole house more accessible to his wheelchair.

Your social services OT can recommend you for a grant from your local authority to cover part of the cost of alterations and Social Services may also contribute. You may be expected to provide the rest yourself, perhaps by extending your mortgage, but you may receive extra help if your income is very low. If you are in privately rented accommodation, your landlord can apply for the grants to do the alterations you need although you may need to work quite hard to persuade him to do them in the first place. If you or your landlord receive a grant, part of it may have to be repaid if the house is sold within a stipulated number of years.

If you are in council housing, the council carry out the alterations using the ordinary housing budget as they are not eligible for grants. In theory, this should not make any difference as the money will come out of the public purse anyway but life is not that simple. If the council supplying social services is not the same one providing your housing, you may find your alterations delayed while the councils argue about which of them should pay. If all else fails, make a fuss (see Chapter 10).

Plan your alterations to your home well ahead for both

bureaucracy and builders are very slow. It is important to plan for any different needs your child may develop in future years as it is difficult to obtain a second grant for further alterations. Grants cannot be paid retrospectively so don't hire an architect or start any building work until the grant is arranged.

Getting items made

If you know a piece of equipment or toy would suit your child but it needs to be specially made or adapted, there may be someone locally who would do the work for you. Schools, colleges and industrial training schemes are often looking for interesting projects for students to tackle and may agree to make or adapt equipment for a local child. The professionals you are working with will often contact them for you. You and your child will probably need to have some contact with the students, both to make the project more meaningful for them and to ensure that what they make is suitable.

14
Is Hospital Really Necessary?

Some hospital admissions are emergencies leaving you no time to plan beforehand or prepare your child. More commonly, though, you will have enough warning to gather your thoughts and possessions. One important, though often overlooked, consideration is 'Does your child really need to go to hospital at all?'

Surgery

Obviously surgery cannot be done at home, but it may be possible for your child's stay to be shorter than originally suggested. Children are often admitted at least one day, maybe more, before the operation. Often this is necessary for preliminary tests to be carried out but sometimes it is just to allow the child to settle in and to ensure he does not eat before the anaesthetic.

If you live reasonably near the hospital and are confident you can 'starve' your child properly, it may be possible for him not to be admitted until the morning of the operation. If the idea appeals to you, talk it over with the surgeon in advance but don't be too disappointed if your suggestion is rejected.

Your child's operation may be necessary but not urgent. If he is already upset by starting school or the arrival of a new baby, you may feel he should be spared further distress for a while. Perhaps he is older and would prefer his operation at a time which does not interfere with cub camp or important exams. If you feel your child could cope better with surgery at a later date, discuss this with his doctor well in advance. Your child already has his life affected by his special needs. It is quite reasonable to try to minimize any further effects as much as possible.

If your child has a condition requiring a succession of operations, you may reach a stage where you have all coped with as much as you can for the time being. If so, ask for the next operation to be postponed for a while. Remember the doctors look primarily at your child's medical condition. It is up to you to remember his emotional well-being and to point out to the doctors anything which may help.

Medical treatment

It can be easier to avoid admissions to hospital if your child only needs medical treatment. Parents throughout the country have proved themselves capable of learning complicated medical and postoperative care including renal dialysis and intravenous drug therapy.

If your child is about to receive treatment in hospital which you feel could possibly be given at home, discuss the situation with your consultant. It is worth pointing out the distress and difficulty caused to you all by a hospital admission as she may be unaware of it, especially if you always look calm and in control. If possible, talk to your doctor well in advance as she may need to discuss the idea with colleagues. It may also take time to organize the necessary equipment and training you will need.

Don't be afraid to change your mind if you decide the task is more than you can handle after all. There is nothing wrong in admitting the responsibility feels too great or the procedures too complicated. Don't be too disappointed either if the idea of home treatment proves unworkable.

Home treatment

If you do agree to carry out complicated treatments at home, it is important to have good support which you can contact day or night. Find out if your GP is involved in the plan and ask whether you should contact him or the hospital if you need advice in the middle of the night. Some children's units have a nursing sister employed to work partly in the community to prevent children being admitted unnecessarily. She may be a good support as may your community (or district) nurse. Make sure you have clear instructions on what might go wrong, what to do if it does, and how quickly you need to act. You need to know what is an emergency and what can wait for the next day.

Speaking from personal experience, we have given intravenous drugs at home. It was far better for the children and for us than having them in hospital but it was still a big emotional strain. My hands shook when I filled the syringes and the wretched air bubbles would not move for me although they always would for someone more experienced. At first, the children were very apprehensive about being treated by us but soon agreed that it was far preferable to being in hospital. We found we understood the treatment far better than when they were in hospital as we were given far more information. We will certainly do it again if the need arises.

Other alternatives

If treatment at home is impossible, discuss with the doctors whether your child needs to be on the ward all the time. If treatment or observations are done in the daytime, could he come home to sleep? If nothing happens during the afternoon, could he come home for a few hours or go to the shops or the park if home is too far away? If he is admitted for tests could he go home while he is awaiting the results rather than sitting around with nothing happening? The shorter the time in hospital can be, the better for the whole family.

15
Going into Hospital

It is now widely accepted that all children need their parents with them as much as possible when they are in hospital. As a result, children's wards now allow unrestricted visiting by parents and most of them allow Mum or Dad to stay overnight, although the facilities available for resident parents vary widely from one hospital to another.

If your child is admitted to a specialist ward rather than a children's one you may need to ask for unrestricted visiting. If you are refused, ask again higher up the hospital hierarchy or contact the National Association for the Welfare of Children in Hospital (NAWCH) for advice.

Visiting

Staying in hospital all the time is easiest to achieve if your child is admitted for just a few days for tests or a simple operation. If he is admitted for a long course of treatment or will have repeated frequent admissions, the rest of the family may not be able to cope with Mum or Dad being away for large periods of time. Your other children may feel neglected or abandoned, while you and your partner may miss the mutual support you can give each other.

There is no easy answer. When you are in hospital, you will feel guilty about the children left behind and when you are at home you will feel guilty you are not in hospital. You must work out the solution which feels best for you but accept that it will not be a perfect answer because there isn't one.

Your presence is particularly important if your child is in isolation. However well-intentioned the nurses are, there will not be enough staff for someone to be with him all the time. The hours will drag without company to counteract the boredom and loneliness.

Even if you cannot be with him all the time, give a high priority to staying with your child all the time for the first day or two while he settles into the routine and the staff become accustomed to his special needs. Also try to be there just before, during and after any unpleasant treatments as that is when his need for you may be greatest. If you are waiting for treatment to happen but need to leave your child for a while, ask the staff not to do anything until you get back. It's unfuriating to sit by your child's bed for ages only to find he is given his injection while you have popped out to the loo.

If you are worried how to cope with visiting, talk to the ward sister or a medical social worker. They may have ideas you would never have thought of. It is occasionally possible for a little brother or sister to stay in hospital too or for the social services to help by finding someone to look after your other children during the day.

Life can be easier if Dad (and Mum too, if appropriate) can have time off work while your child is in hospital. Although this is not always possible, employers are often far more sympathetic and flexible than you might expect so it is worth asking. Even if time off is out of the question, more flexible hours may be possible.

If the hospital is a long way from home, there may be no alternative to one parent being resident as travelling backwards and forwards each day would be impossible or too expensive. When faced with a very long admission (several weeks or even months) some parents stay at the hospital part of the week but spend the rest of the week at home. Other couples share the load, perhaps with Mum staying during the week while Dad goes at weekends. If you cannot visit for a while, keep in touch by phone or letter. An older child can be left coins for the phone so he can call home whenever he wants.

If your child is in a local hospital, it is possible to visit every day but sleep at home. You can also share the visiting with other relatives – perhaps Nanny or Grandad can go sometimes to give you time with the rest of the family. Don't forget your child may also welcome visits from his brothers and sisters, school friends or teachers.

Communications

Don't assume that the hospital will automatically know how to cope with your child's special needs. Even children with the same condition often require different care or handling. You may need to demonstrate the best methods of feeding, dressing or lifting.

You may have to explain things more than once. Just telling one of the nurses is often not enough as staff go on and off duty. A note on the locker or bed is a good way of reminding staff of any special information like your child's special sign for the toilet or the time you will be coming back to the ward.

Don't assume the hospital will have all the special equipment your child needs. If he has a special chair or special eating utensils, take them with you. If you are in doubt, phone the ward first to check. I know of one girl with severe cerebral palsy who spent a whole week confined to bed because there was no suitable chair to enable her to sit in the playroom with the other children.

Ward rounds

A formal ward round where the consultant visits each bed accompanied by a retinue of nurses, junior doctors, medical students and other people can be daunting. If the consultant talks to the people with him all the time, you may feel awkward about saying anything. Don't be: try to pretend the others don't exist and ask all the questions you need answered.

Very, very occasionally an unfeeling doctor may discuss your child's condition as if he wasn't there – perhaps referring to his future deterioration or impending death. If you feel the situation is intolerable, say so. Ask them to stop and continue their conversation elsewhere. You are not being unreasonable – they are. You and your child have a right to be treated with respect and understanding.

Making life better

Hospitals are hot places so wear cool comfortable clothes yourself. Take something to do as hours can drag when your child wants you there for security but does not need you to play with him. Frequent interruptions and the dullness of mind which appears to accompany hospital visiting make the best choices of occupation those which require little concentration.

Say 'Hello' to the other parents on the ward. They are probably feeling just as lonely as you. You can give each other mutual support by chatting, going for coffee together or keeping an eye on each other's child while one of you has a break.

The arrival of the post breaks up the hospital day. Whereas a child having his tonsils out will be inundated with get-well cards, a child with regular admissions may receive none at all as being in hospital is no longer a novelty. If necessary, remind friends and relatives to send letters and cards as your child will feel left out if nothing arrives for him.

Going home

All the literature about children in hospital tells you to expect a reaction from your child when he comes home. He may be extra tired from missed sleep and show signs of insecurity. Common sense tells you that your other children may be extra demanding or clingy too if you have been away from them.

Less spoken of, but just as likely, is a strong reaction of your own. Finally getting your child home can release the tension of the previous days resulting in floods of tears or outbursts of anger. You may feel insecure at losing the support of the hospital staff if your child's condition needs continuing care. If you have been resident in the hospital, you are probably also very tired as few parents sleep well on the ward.

Life will return to normal eventually. Realize you have all been through a tough time and allow yourselves time to recover.

16
Getting a Break

Looking after any child is hard work so all parents welcome a rest from time to time. If your child requires more care or supervision than average, your need for an occasional break from caring will be even greater.

Some parents are reluctant to leave their special child at all. They fear he would be unhappy without them or that other people cannot give him such high quality care as they do. Be careful if you feel this way as it can lead to problems eventually. With no rest from constant caring, stress and physical tiredness can build up until you find you can no longer cope. Your marriage and your other children can also suffer from lack of attention.

Don't assume that leaving your child with someone else is automatically bad for him. It can widen his horizons and give him some independence from you. One day you may need someone else to take over if you are ill. Your child will cope much better then if he is already used to being away from you and knows his substitute carers.

Baby-sitters

Most parents use a baby-sitter occasionally to allow them to go out, leaving the children safe in their own surroundings. Relatives, teenage girls and baby-sitting circles meet most parents' needs. If your child needs extra care you may find it more difficult to find someone able to cope.

In some areas of the country, there is a home-sitting scheme which supplies sitters for people caring for handicapped or sick relatives. This may be provided through social services or a voluntary scheme. Ask around to see if there is one in your area – your health visitor or social worker may know or you can ask other parents or your local branch of the Carers National Association.

If your local college runs a nursery nursing course, one of their students may like to baby-sit for your child to gain experience. Try contacting the organizer of the course via the college.

Paying someone to baby-sit may be too expensive to allow you to go out much, but reciprocal baby-sitting arrangements keep the costs down. If you cannot join an ordinary baby-sitting circle, could you swap baby-sitting with another parent of a child with special needs?

Respite care

Whereas a baby-sitter cares for your child at home, respite care involves him being looked after elsewhere – either with another family or in a hospital or residential home. Respite care schemes exist in many parts of the country under various names and are organized either by social services or by a local voluntary group. Some, but not all, limit the care you can use each year.

Parents vary in the amount of respite care they want. Some use it one day a week, perhaps to simplify shopping. Some use it irregularly while others prefer regular breaks such as one weekend a month. Many families use respite care to allow them a week or fortnight's holiday without their handicapped child.

Although you may feel guilty at the initial idea of sending your child to strangers, don't forget that he will benefit as well. Your child will enjoy the attention and his horizons will be widened by seeing new people and places. He may also enjoy feeling independent from you, especially if he is of an age when he would be doing things on his own if circumstances were different. In any case, he will benefit from his parents being relaxed and refreshed when he returns home.

With another family

This type of respite care is different from fostering. You are not giving up any of your rights as a parent and you are not putting your child 'into care'. You are just sharing the workload.

The carers are people who realize how great the strain of caring for a handicapped child can be and want to help by taking a child into their home for a while. Don't let their apparent ability to cope make you feel inadequate. Remember they only look after him for a short time so it is easy for them to give him more attention than you reasonably could. They start fresh, not exhausted, and can leave the housework until he returns home.

Some parents say 'They'll never find anyone who wants to take my child.' Don't let this worry prevent you applying for respite care. Some carers are willing to take very difficult children and are not deterred by incontinence, fits, difficult behaviour or total helplessness. Some actually prefer the more difficult children as they enjoy the challenge and feel they are helping more.

Residential units

In some areas there is a hostel or residential unit exclusively used to provide a break for parents. In others, one or two respite care places may be reserved in a residential home. You usually have to book in advance unless it is an emergency. Because staff work duty rotas, your child may have less opportunity to build new relationships than he would in a family. Also, he is less likely to be the centre of attention, which you may consider an advantage or a disadvantage.

Such schemes offer your child good substitute care and a change of environment. I have heard of many children who look forward to their visits. If your child has particular difficulties like running away or severe fits at night, you may feel more confident leaving him where there are staff on duty day and night and good locks on the door.

For older children, short-term stays in a hostel or home can provide a useful introduction to living away from home. In fact, many residential units like to build up to long-term admission by a series of visits and short stays unless an emergency forces an immediate move.

Hospital

Sometimes children are admitted to an ordinary children's ward to give their parents a break. Many parents view this as a poor substitute to other forms of respite care and use it only as a last resort. It is usually offered to severely handicapped children who need a great deal of nursing care such as suction, tube-feeding or regular turning through the night. The main concern of parents is that the physical care is excellent but there is insufficient stimulation.

Obviously it is distressing to put your child into a situation where you feel he will not receive the same high quality of care which you give him. However, it is better to let your child go into hospital for a few days than to struggle on with no break when you need one. If you collapse from exhaustion or the family disintegrates, the effects on your child will be much worse.

71

Who can use respite care?

Most schemes are only available for severely handicapped children and some are limited to mentally handicapped children. Receipt of Attendance Allowance is often used as a guide to eligibility. Rules are, of course, there to be broken or bent and some schemes are more flexible than they seem at first glance.

If you feel you need respite care but your child is not eligible, apply anyway. The worst they can do is say 'No'. Explain why you feel you need the help and ask your health visitor, social worker or other professional to support your application. Even if respite care is not available, it is sometimes possible to use short-term fostering in a similar way if your home situation is suffering.

Helen House and Martin House

A special type of respite care is offered by Helen House and Martin House if your child has a life-threatening illness or progressive disorder such as cancer, Batten's Disease or muscular dystrophy. Your whole family can stay at the house so you have a break from housework and caring without being separated from your child. Both houses also offer ordinary respite care, if you prefer, plus long-term support throughout your child's illness. (See Chapter 23.)

Holidays together

If you want to go on holiday together as a family, your child's special needs may complicate life. There are many different organizations offering holidays for the disabled but I am not listing them here for lack of space and because the information would rapidly become out of date.

The Holiday Care Service offers free advice on holidays for people with special needs. They can give you information on accommodation, transport, inclusive holidays and possible sources of financial help. Your voluntary organization may have ideas too and RADAR produce information leaflets about holidays and travel. Some of the larger charities for handicapped and sick children have suitable holiday accommodation available at reasonable rates.

Holidays apart

A holiday for your child without you can do more than just give you a break. It can give him independence and the confidence to know he can manage away from you. It can also allow him to mix with other children with similar problems which he may welcome if he feels isolated and different.

Once again the Holiday Care Service can give you information on this type of holiday. Ask your voluntary organization too as they may organize holidays for unaccompanied children or know of someone who does. Schools sometimes organize holidays or residential field trips although you may need to push hard for your child to be included if he is at ordinary school. The Girl Guide and Boy Scout organizations run camps for their members and usually try hard to include all the children in their group even if they have special needs.

A pilgrimage to Lourdes can be a very special form of holiday. The Across Trust organizes groups which travel there by Jumbulance – large coaches equipped with beds as well as seats. My eldest son went with them when he was ten and thoroughly enjoyed it. Also, the Handicapped Children's Pilgrimage Trust takes a large group of children to Lourdes each Easter. Both organizations will consider any sick or handicapped child whether Roman Catholic or not.

17

When you Can't Cope any More

This chapter is not written from a 'holier than thou' position. I am not some superior being who can cope with all the difficulties life throws my way while looking immaculate and producing piles of beautiful iced cakes for the school fair. Quite the reverse – I have hit rock bottom so often I am beginning to know it quite well. The ideas presented here are not just theories: they have been learnt the hard way to the accompaniment of a good many tears.

Your child's special needs produce extra work and stress for you. As a result, more work, more stress or less sleep can bring you to breaking point more easily than if your life was less demanding initially. Everyone has physical and emotional limits, and there is no shame in admitting you have reached them.

Your low patch may be only temporary. Perhaps you know you will feel better once your period has started, the children have gone back to school or your cold has cleared up. Sometimes, though, there is no relief in sight. From your position of abject misery, the future looks unbearable.

Once you have admitted to yourself that you have reached the end of your tether, try telling your partner. You may need to repeat yourself several times before the message sinks in as he or she may be reluctant to face the truth. You could also talk to a close friend or one of the professionals – anyone who is a good listener and likely to be supportive. Talking about your situation can help you sort out your ideas so you can decide what to do next. Remember the situation is unlikely to improve permanently if everything is left as it is.

Visit your doctor

It is worth telling your GP how low you feel. She can check there is no medical reason for you not coping. Anaemia, period problems, chronically blocked sinuses and many other relatively minor problems can wear you down and contribute to your tiredness. Ask her about any worries you have about your health so she can either treat them or reassure you that all is well.

You may be reluctant to visit your doctor in case she prescribes tranquillizers, sleeping pills or antidepressants. Please don't let that stop you. Doctors are far less willing to give those types of medicine than they were in the past. If yours does suggest drugs, ask what they will do, how long you will need them, what side-effects they have and whether they are addictive. Only agree to take them if you are happy with the answers. Don't feel guilty if you need to take antidepressants for a while; sometimes they can help lift the gloom enough for you to sort out a long-term solution.

Making a breathing space

What you need now is a breathing space. Take off as much pressure as you can. Even if none of the ideas in 'Getting a Break' (Chapter 16) are feasible right now, try to arrange things at home to be as relaxed as possible. Forget about cakes for the school fair, give them a packet of biscuits instead. Plan easy meals and postpone non-urgent appointments until you feel better. Put yourself first for once. Your needs matter and should not always be ignored.

Use this time to think about why you have reached this stage and how you can stop yourself getting there again. Share this process with your partner as it is important that the solutions are agreeable to both of you. Remember, the situations likely to have caused your crisis are too much work, too much stress, too little sleep or a combination of all three. All these cause tiredness which reduces your ability to cope, making everything an effort and easily transforming molehills into mountains. That is why the breathing space is so important: it relieves your tiredness so you can think more clearly.

You will know if you are physically tired but you may not realize straight away that you are emotionally tired. I know I didn't. Signs to watch for are feeling panic at the slightest thing or feeling that if something else went wrong you either wouldn't cope or wouldn't care. You may also cry more easily or be more inclined to shout at the children.

What's gone wrong?

There are many reasons why your workload may have increased. Perhaps your child's condition has deteriorated so he needs feeding or is incontinent. Perhaps he has grown so big that lifting him is now exhausting. The changes may have happened so slowly that you have not realized until now how much extra work they are causing.

Perhaps your child's condition has stayed the same but you now receive less help. The parents or in-laws you once relied on for help may now be too old or sick to help or may even have died. A previously very supportive friend may have moved away or your husband's job may have changed so he works longer hours or goes on business trips. These and similar situations can leave you coping alone far more than you did before or mean you have fewer breaks from caring.

Maybe the extra work is nothing to do with your special child. Caring for a new baby or a frail, elderly relative takes time and energy. Although commitments outside home can provide a welcome break from routine they can, if you are not careful, build up to more than you can handle.

Nearly all the situations which increase your workload will also increase the stress you are under. In fact, most changes in life are stressful, even the pleasant ones like moving to a better house. Think carefully about all the changes which have happened to you in the last year. Remember that a number of seemingly minor events can combine to cause almost as much stress as one major catastrophe.

There are many other reasons why you might be under stress. At various times I have been worn down by worrying about when I should take the boys to the doctor, about their problems at school, about leaking roofs and broken washing machines and about my own health. Money, or rather the lack of it, can cause worries too. Perhaps one of you has been made redundant so you face a big drop in income. Perhaps you have to pay extra for trips to hospital, large repair bills or increased mortgage payments.

Working out a plan

Once you have thought out all the reasons you have become so low, the next step is to decide what action to take. You won't be able to remove all the problems but it may be possible to reduce some of them and to improve your ability to cope with those that are left.

When you are considering what action to take, think of as many possibilities as you can, not just the obvious ones. As well as trying to lessen the workload, look for ways to make more opportunities to relax or make better use of those that you already have. Remember it is often more relaxing to do something else which takes your mind off your worries than it is to do nothing at all. The rest of this book should help you come up with some ideas. You may also find it helpful to talk to your health visitor, social worker or someone else who knows what help is available locally. Your local Citizens Advice Bureau may be able to offer advice on money problems.

To give you an idea of what I mean, let's look at the list I produced when I became really low. The items beyond my control were the boys having cystic fibrosis and the deaths of Steve's parents which left me with less support and help. The other problems were:

(a) Steve was working overtime and making frequent business trips, often quite long and at short notice.

(b) The children were older and staying up later so we had less time to ourselves in the evenings.

(c) I had no interests to take me out of the house during the day or take my mind off our problems.

(d) We lived a long way from the hospital which made visiting difficult.

(e) Matthew was very unhappy at school.

Our first idea was for Steve to change his job so we could move nearer the hospital. Although that would have solved some of the problems, it would have created others as we would have had no friends to support us in the new area. In the end, we stayed where we were but Steve stopped going away and working overtime. His employers were very understanding when the situation was explained to them.

We also took positive action about Matthew's school problems instead of just worrying about them. We arranged for a regular baby-sitter so we could go out once a week. I started writing regularly and helping at our local toy library, both of which helped relieve my boredom and frustration. I found the family supported me in this now they understood how much I needed other interests.

Writing that down makes it sound trivially simple whereas it really took several months of thinking, looking at alternatives, making false starts and getting upset. Don't expect any overnight improvements but you will probably feel better once you know you are trying to find a solution.

Making hard decisions

The right solution for you may not necessarily be the easiest one for everyone else. An interest outside the home may provide a necessary break for you but the children may resent having a little less attention. Only you can weigh up the merits of the different alternatives but don't forget to put your own needs fairly high on the list of priorities. Like me, you may find other members of the family feel better about any inconvenience to them if they understand how important the change is for you.

It is easy to take on more work than you can handle but it is harder to admit you need to stop doing something. It can hurt both you and the people you are letting down and can leave you feeling guilty, especially if you feel you should have been able to manage. Don't be too hard on yourself if you find you need to give up some of the demands on your time. There is a limit to the amount anyone can do and there is no shame in admitting you have passed it.

You will probably feel particularly guilty if you find you can no longer cope with your child's care. Perhaps you are exhausted from lifting him or from turning him every two hours through the night. Perhaps his behaviour is so difficult that you are trapped at home, unable to even go to the shops. There is no shame in admitting you cannot manage – you are not an inadequate parent, just one facing demands which are too great. Don't let fear that your child may have to leave home prevent you admitting you need help. That is only one possible solution. Respite care or better equipment may make enough difference for you to be able to cope again. If your child is very dependent on you and likely to remain so, you probably will have to consider alternative care for him as you grow older. There is nothing wrong with admitting it now and starting to plan towards it.

If you are faced with really difficult decisions, it can help to talk about them with someone who understands what you are facing: another parent, a friend or one of the professionals you deal with. You will feel less guilty about your eventual decision if someone you trust agrees it is the right one.

18

Alternatives to Care at Home

A long time ago, many handicapped children were placed in institutions where they lived a life very different to that experienced in an ordinary family. Their parents were expected to behave as if nothing had gone wrong while those who chose to keep their children at home received little support. The situation today is very different as parents are encouraged to care for their sick or handicapped children themselves. However, not all of us manage to cope indefinitely.

If you find you can no longer care for your child, you are not alone. Life is very unfair and some people find, as you have, that they are faced with too many problems at once. Just like you, they still love their children. Sometimes it takes more courage and love to admit that someone else can do better than you than it does to struggle on while failing to cope properly.

There are many reasons why your child may need to live away from home either temporarily or permanently. Perhaps lack of local facilities means boarding school is the only way he can achieve his full potential. Maybe problems with your own health have left you physically unable to cope with his care. You may be one of the many families who manage all right while their child is small but find life increasingly difficult as the years go by. Lifting a heavy teenager is far harder than moving a toddler. Difficult behaviour from a child of two is much easier to handle than the same behaviour when your child is 14 and you yourselves are twelve years older.

If you find you can no longer give your child all the care and special help he needs, you may eventually need to love him enough to let him go or, at least, to share him. This is a very painful decision to make but you are not being cruel and unloving to consider it – just realistic. Finding out the options available does not commit you to parting from him – it gives you the information you need to make the right decisions for his future.

To find out about alternatives to living at home, ask your social worker or another professional you trust. Even if they do not have all the information you need, they should know where to get it. Your voluntary society may also have useful ideas. If you hear of a school or home which sounds suitable, you can contact it yourself for further information; you don't have to channel your enquiry through a professional.

You may find it hard to persuade the authorities your child needs to live away from home, especially as this arrangement can be very expensive for them. It can help to have the support of your doctor, health visitor or social worker or (in the case of boarding school) of an education expert.

Shared care

Sharing the care of your child with other people may be the most acceptable alternative for you. Your child spends part of his life with you and the rest in a residential unit or boarding school where the staff have the time, energy and experience to help him gain new skills and independence. The long, regular breaks from caring allows you and the rest of your family time to rest and gather strength so you can cope again when your child comes home.

Residential care

At one time residential care meant a large impersonal ward in a Victorian institution which concentrated on the physical care of its residents with little thought being given to their emotional needs. Thankfully such places are gradually being phased out.

Residential care for children is now provided in much smaller homes. Whereas the large institutions were usually in isolated areas, these small homes are often in ordinary residential areas where the children can be part of the local community. Many are in ordinary houses, indistinguishable from others in the road.

The various homes differ widely in size and organization. Some are run to a fixed daily routine with meals arriving from a kitchen the children rarely visit. Others aim for a more homely atmosphere with flexible routines and staff eating with the children. It is now common practice in most homes for each child to have one member of staff as his key worker. She acts as a substitute parent and keeps in contact with the school, buys clothes and generally shows a special interest in her particular child.

Visit any homes which may be suitable for your child before you make any decisions about his future; two places which sound similar on paper may differ widely in atmosphere. Exactly which aspects of the home are most important to you will vary according to your child's special needs. If he is hyperactive your main concern may be whether the garden is adequately fenced whereas, if he is extremely physically dependent but mentally alert, you may need reassurance that his mind will be kept occupied. However, always try to see the whole building and meet as many of the staff and children as possible. Ask as many questions as you wish – your decision will affect your child's whole future so it is important that you have all the information you need.

Most specialized residential homes are full so you may have to put your child's name on a waiting list. In the meantime, you will have to continue at home as best you can or accept a less than suitable placement temporarily. Sometimes a social worker or doctor can speed placement if the situation at home has become extremely difficult.

Family placements

In the past it was considered impossible to place children with special needs in foster or adoptive homes but more recent work has shown that even very severely handicapped or dying children can be placed with families. As a result, you may be offered a foster home for your child if you cannot care for him yourself for a while. Also fostering or adoption may be suggested if your child is unlikely to return to live with you, even if he is already in residential care.

If your child only needs a temporary placement while you are ill in hospital or having a baby, you may be happier knowing he is staying with another family rather than in a residential home. However, if you have found you cannot cope with him, you may be unwilling to let another family try. Perhaps you feel unwilling to burden another family with the disruptions yours has endured. More possibly though, you are frightened that someone else will cope where you did not. If your child is in a residential home you can say to yourself that he is impossible to care for in a normal family. If he is successfully fostered, you will have to face the fact that someone else has succeeded where you failed.

Don't be too hard on yourself if this happens. Remember that the foster parents have chosen to take your child knowing the problems they will face. They are free from the emotional reactions you have endured and, most important of all, they do not have the other problems you face. Their life situation is different from yours. If they were placed in exactly your position they might not cope either.

Another fear you may have about fostering is that the foster parents will replace you in your child's affections. Certainly he is likely to call them 'Mum' and 'Dad', especially if he is quite young when he goes there and he is staying a long time. He will grow to love the people who care for him each day but love is not an exclusive thing. When we start to love a new person, we do not have to stop loving the one before. If he is permanently living with someone else, his relationship with you will change but that does not mean it will die.

Helping your child to move

If your child's move away from home is a planned one rather than the sudden result of a family crisis, there is much you can do to lessen his fears about it. Talk to him about the changes ahead, emphasizing that he is not being sent away because he has been naughty. If possible take him to see his new home at least once, preferably more often, before he moves. If you can obtain photos of the new place and the people there, these will provide something concrete to talk about when you discuss the future together.

Only tell the truth about what is happening. Don't promise he will come home if you know he won't. On the other hand, if he is coming back, at least for visits, reassure him by leaving things ready for his return. Give realistic promises about your visits, letters and phone calls and keep them.

Perhaps your child is so severely handicapped that you think he has no understanding. Talk about the future anyway. He may understand more than you expect and if he doesn't you will only have wasted a little breath.

Sharing his past

At home you are your child's link with his past. You know how much he weighed when he was born and all the other facts which add up to make him who he is. His new carers will not be able to tell him such things unless you provide the information.

If he is only going away briefly, perhaps while you have an operation or until the end of term at his residential school, it is enough to provide him with photos of the family and some background information about life at home. Please label the photographs clearly if your child's memory is poor or he cannot speak well. Then his carers can help keep his memories alive by talking to him about familiar things.

If he is leaving home permanently, it is good for him to have much more information. Making a scrapbook or album together about his life with you is a positive way of helping him which may also lessen the guilt you will probably feel in those last few weeks.

Into the book put all the information you can about your child: details of his birth, early life, special events, etc. Include photos and other souvenirs which seem appropriate. If you cannot bear to part with any of these, consider having copies made. Documents can be photocopied and new prints can be made from photographs even if you do not have the negatives. Try to include any information he may need when he is older such as family medical details. It can be embarrassing for an adult to have to explain why he is ignorant of his family background.

If you cannot face making the book yourself or his move happens too rapidly to allow you to do it, sort out the information and material anyway. Then pass it on, suitably labelled, to his new carers for them to deal with. Showing this care for his future well-being is a positive way to demonstrate that you still love him even though circumstances force him to live away from you.

Visits

Unless you are making a complete break with your child, you will visit him in his new home. These visits are important to maintain your relationship with him, especially if you plan to have him home again eventually. If he is fostered, your visits are technically called 'access'. The frequency of your visits is usually decided before your child moves. Even if the foster family or residential home encourage you to visit at any time, they would probably welcome some warning of your arrival just as you would if someone were visiting you. In fact, the best guide to how to behave on such occasions is to mentally put yourself in the place of the people you are visiting.

Try to be more willing to compliment than criticize even though it is hard to see your child cared for by someone else who does not do everything the same way as you did. If you are worried about some aspect of his care, ask about it in as friendly a way as possible. It often helps to praise some other point before you broach the more difficult subject.

You are certain to feel awkward the first few times you visit but don't let that put you off going. As you adjust to the new people and the new situation you will feel more relaxed. Your child may react at first with wild excitement, floods of tears or even by ignoring you completely. He too will gradually adjust to the fact that you now visit and go away again.

When you visit, it can be tempting to take your child out and pretend that everything is as it was. Of course outings will be fun for him but don't forget to take an interest in his new life as well. If he is able to, let him be your host and show you round.

The relationship between natural parents and foster parents is a difficult one. There is nothing equivalent to guide you in how to act but it is important to try hard to get on with each other for it can make a great difference to your child's happiness. If his foster placement is successful he will grow to love his substitute parents as well as loving you and he will be unhappy if the important adults in his life do not like each other. As long as you all consider each other's feelings everything should go well. Try to show an interest in the other children in the foster family – who can easily feel left out during access visits – your efforts will be appreciated by the foster parents.

After he has gone

Not everyone will understand your motives in letting your child go. Even if some people have been urging you for years to put him in a home, there will be others swift to criticize if you actually do so. Try to grow a thicker skin so you can ignore their comments. What right have they to find fault with you? What makes them so sure they would cope any better if they were in your situation?

If you have other children, they may be very upset by the absence of their brother or sister even if they were always grumbling about him or her. They may feel guilty that they caused your child to be sent away or worry that they too may have to leave eventually.

It is important that they know in advance that your special child is leaving and have a chance to say goodbye. Let them know (and if possible see) where he is going. Explain that it is no one's fault that he must go but just the consequence of his special needs which you as a family can no longer satisfy. Although you can point out that they do not have those needs so will not need to go away, don't be surprised if your other children need extra attention and cuddles to reassure them of their security.

Adoption and custodianship

If your child lives with foster parents, they take over the daily care of your child but you keep your legal rights as his parent. It is sometimes possible for the local authority to take over your parental rights. If they try to do so against your wishes it is important that you consult a solicitor straight away, preferably one experienced in child care law.

Long-term fostering offers no security to your child or his foster parents. Custodianship formalizes their relationship, granting the foster parents some of your legal rights (like choosing schools and consenting to operations) while your child still remains legally part of your family. It could be a good idea if you are happy for your child to remain permanently with his foster parents and they wish to make a commitment to him without adopting him. It gives them more control over his life while acknowledging his family ties.

Adoption breaks all your child's legal ties with your family. He takes the name of his new parents and is legally as much their child as if he had been born to them. At one time, adoption also meant no further contact with your family but that is not always so today. Some adoptive parents do keep in contact with their child's first family. The amount of contact varies from occasional letters and photographs to regular visits. This type of open adoption is more likely to happen if your child was initially fostered by the adopters so you already know each other or if your child is old enough for a complete break not to be in his best interests.

It is hard to give up your child to someone else's care. Allowing him to be adopted can be even harder as it forces you to accept he will never return. However, it may be that the greatest gift you can give him is the freedom to become a complete member of his new family; the death of your dreams may provide him with the absolute security he needs. Remember, adoption is only a legal ceremony. No court can ever change the past. Your child will always have the characteristics he inherited from you. It will always be you who gave him life.

PART FOUR
Family Matters

19
Taking the Strain off your Marriage

According to some experts, divorce is more common among couples with a handicapped child. It's a frightening thought, but it does *not* mean your marriage is doomed to failure. No one knows how many of those broken marriages would have ended in divorce even if all the children had been perfectly all right. Perhaps the extra stress just makes it harder to limp along in a partnership which is already unhappy for other reasons.

However, your child's problems can place an extra strain on your relationship. Nearly all the parents who helped with my research admitted their marriage had been through some bad patches as they came to terms with their new situation. They argued and shouted or failed to talk to each other much at all. However, most had worked through the bad times to a greater understanding so don't assume you are heading for the divorce courts just because your relationship does not seem too good at the moment.

Facing facts

Not everyone reacts the same way to bad news; individual personality and upbringing affect behaviour. In particular, women are more likely to cry openly and want to talk about what has happened. Men are brought up to put on a brave face and struggle through their difficulties without the emotional release of tears. Faced with a weeping wife, many men feel they should be even more stoic and unemotional in order to support her through her distress.

This contrasting behaviour can be very upsetting after you have just learnt your child has problems. However happy you were before, you may find your differing reactions make you feel isolated from each other and think you are growing apart. I know I did at one stage and it was a frightening feeling.

The solution suggested by parent after parent is to talk to each other. This is not as easy as it seems if you have lost the habit. My husband says my plaintive cries of 'Talk to me about it!' left him in confusion. By then, he was so accustomed to suppressing his emotions, he was no longer sure of them himself, let alone able to talk about them. We kept trying and it gradually got easier – as I hope it will for you.

Remember, this is a shared experience, so share the heartache and the joys. Talk together, cry together, laugh together for otherwise you add the pain of loneliness to all the other hurts. Sharing your worst fears with each other won't make them go away but it might make them easier to handle.

The overtime syndrome

Unless Mum goes to work, she is the one left, literally, holding the baby. Her emotions are probably in turmoil during those early months. Guilt, rejection, fear and love may intermingle in the confusion. The sheer responsibility can seem terrifying and she may feel trapped by the situation, any plans she had for returning to work shattered by the new reality.

Mum has to face the facts every day. Hospital visits, physiotherapy, medicines and special care combine to make it impossible for her to deny the problems exist, to pretend that all is well. Dad is in a different situation: his emotions may be in a similar turmoil but he sees his child less frequently and is less involved in the caring and treatment. As well as making it more difficult for him to build up a relationship with his special son or daughter, this also makes it easier for him to deny the problem exists.

Whereas Mum cannot escape, Dad can: work offers alternative stress to take his mind off the worries at home. Many Dads start working hours and hours of overtime after they learn their child has problems. It keeps them away from the worries of home and saves them facing up to the situation – at least, that's how their wives view it.

Dad probably sees it differently. He is upset to see his wife working so hard and worrying but he cannot take away the problems. It makes sense to him that he should earn more money – after all, there are probably extra expenses now and he can, at least, relieve the financial worries even though he feels powerless to do anything else.

If you are in the overtime syndrome, talk together about how to deal with it. Do you really need that extra money? Would cutting back on expenditure solve your money worries while allowing the two of you to spend more time together? Perhaps money is not really the root of the problem. Maybe Dad's job is just very demanding and he fears he may lose it if he does not work so hard. If that is really true, perhaps he is in the wrong job for your new situation. Changing jobs is a drastic step but sometimes it is worth doing.

Sharing the care

As well as sharing your feelings, share the practical problems as well. Some employers are very understanding about time off for clinic visits so it is always worth asking. The worst that can happen is a refusal. Even if Dad cannot attend all the appointments, it is good if he can get to the most important ones. With two people listening, you are less likely to miss or forget important information and the travelling and waiting is more bearable with company.

If Mum feels very protective towards this special child of yours, be careful not to let that protectiveness push Dad out of the picture. It's no good her complaining later that he never helps if, for months, she has given him the impression that she doesn't want him to.

Make time for each other

Your marriage is important and justifies time and effort. If you can manage it, give yourselves an occasional break to be together without the children. Even if money is tight, could you just go for a walk together while someone baby-sits for a little while? Several parents said they use some of their child's attendance allowance for an occasional meal out which allows them to recharge their batteries so they can continue to cope.

After our own bad patch came to a head and we started talking more, we decided to do something together. As we live by the sea we spent our spare cash on an elderly dinghy and learnt to sail. It's worked wonders for us, providing time together and something else to talk about. On a rough day, it drives all other worries out of our heads as we struggle to keep it upright!

A boat probably is not the answer for you but do consider doing something together, preferably something which demands sufficient concentration to stop you worrying about home. Learning to dance is one idea as you trample on each others toes if your mind wanders. Evening classes can be fun and so can sports like badminton. Even if lack of baby-sitters makes going out impossible, why not do something together at home rather than watching hours of TV.

Sex

There is more to marriage than sex but it is important. If you have a happy, fulfilling sex life together, it will help you to be happy the rest of the time too. There are two main ways your child's problems can upset this situation.

First, fear of having another sick or handicapped child can leave you really frightened of another pregnancy. Mum, in particular, can be so worried about this that she is reluctant to make love at all. Total abstinence is, of course, the most effective form of birth control but it can leave you both feeling frustrated and less close.

The solution is good contraception – ask your GP or Family Planning Clinic for advice. Sterilization of one or other of you can give complete peace of mind but is only worth considering if you are absolutely positive you will never want another child. Don't rush into a decision without careful thought because the procedure should be regarded as irreversible.

The other way your child's problems may affect your sex life is that it may take so much time and energy that you feel the precious hours you get in bed should be spent asleep. I sympathize but don't forget love-making can be very relaxing. If you sleep better afterwards, the few hours left may do you more good than if you hadn't bothered. Remember, too, that there is no law restricting sex to the bedroom during the hours of darkness. There's nothing wrong with the living room on Saturday afternoon while Granny has taken the children to the park . . .

20

Brothers and Sisters

Next to yourselves, the people who will be most affected by your child's special needs are his brothers and sisters or, as professional jargon calls them, his siblings.

Those who refer to siblings also talk of a phenomenon called sibling rivalry. This is a fancy name for behaviour like kicking your brother under the table, complaining that your sister has a bigger bit of cake and loudly declaring 'It was him!' when it wasn't. Unless you were an only child, you can probably remember many similar examples from your own childhood.

Let's be realistic. There is no law which says brothers and sisters must like each other. Some never do; some are devoted to each other. Mostly, there is a love/hate relationship between the different children in a family so one minute they are fiercely loyal to each other and the next they are bickering and squabbling so much that you could cheerfully knock their heads together. If that is the case in an ordinary family, how can we hope for anything better if we add a child with special needs? In fact, the situation can easily become worse because of the extra care and attention that that child requires.

Fairness is important

Children demand fair treatment from their parents. They want to know they are as important to Mum and Dad as their brothers and sisters are. If one child appears to receive the lion's share of the attention, the others look for ways to even the balance. Unfortunately, one of the quickest ways to make parents take notice is to be naughty. From a child's viewpoint, a smack on the behind may be better than being totally ignored.

Don't jump to the conclusion that all your other children's naughty or strange behaviour is because they have a special brother or sister. They might just be going through an awkward phase or fighting for independence. However, it is important to consider whether they are feeling jealous or left out.

Try to look at the situation through their eyes. Does Dad always come home and kiss your special child first? Do you make more fuss

93

when your spastic child holds a spoon for three seconds than when his sister gets a gold star for her handwriting? Did you fail to watch your son come last at sports day because his sister had to attend hospital for a routine check? It is so easy for even very good parents to get things out of balance without realizing it.

Jealousy is a natural emotion, and bringing such feelings into the open can help make them easier to handle. If you admit that you felt jealous when you were young, your other children may be able to talk more easily about being jealous of their brother or sister. Once you know the problem is there and they realize you understand, the situation is likely to improve. Don't make your other children feel guilty for being jealous or expect them to feel grateful for being normal and healthy.

Children need time

All your children need your time, not just the one who is handicapped or sick. Try to organize yourself to spend a little time regularly and without interruption with each child. That might sound daunting but don't forget you can have good chats while you are ironing, washing up or travelling. Younger children can enjoy your company while 'helping' you with the chores. Bedtime can also be a good time for extra attention.

Special occasions matter so you should attach a high importance to attending school open days, Brownie enrolments and similar events. Your other children have their lives affected by their brother's or sister's extra needs so why should the situation not be reversed sometimes? These events are important so, if necessary, you should leave your special child behind even if he makes a fuss about being left with a baby-sitter.

If it is available, respite care can provide you with the time to give your other children extra attention as well as the opportunity to go on outings and activities which would otherwise be impossible. It may be worth using respite care for their sakes even though you personally could manage without it.

Sharing

A favourite phrase of the professionals is 'A handicapped child means a handicapped family'. I think that is too black a statement but it is true that your special child's problems are, in a way, the whole family's problems. They affect all of you to some extent so it is only fair that everyone should understand them.

Explain his problems to your other children as fully as you can. In particular, if you need to expect different standards of behaviour from them than you do for their brother or sister, make sure they understand the reasons for it. Obviously young children will need a very simple explanation but don't forget to upgrade it as they grow older. Remember that, just like you, they will not understand everything the first time so be prepared to repeat your explanations and be open to questions.

If your children are older than your special child, it is important to explain what is wrong from the earliest days for they will see your grief and it will frighten them. They can easily feel pushed out of the family circle if they do not understand what is happening. If the new baby has to stay in hospital, try to involve them in any way you can. Let them visit the ward if possible. Perhaps they could draw pictures to hang by the cot or you could take photos of the baby for them to have at home.

Similarly, if your child needs frequent hospital admissions, it is important to consider the needs of his brothers and sisters when you decide how much you stay with him. Otherwise they can dread the thought of hospital as a place which spirits away Mum or Dad as well as their brother or sister. Sharing visiting between Mum and Dad, spending school hours in hospital and evenings at home and letting brothers and sisters visit with you, are all ways of easing the situation.

Family problems need to be tackled by the whole family. Look for ways to involve your other children in the care of their brother or sister but beware of making helping a burden. Perhaps they would enjoy learning sign language or doing physiotherapy even if rather incompetently. Help them to understand why sometimes your special child should be allowed to struggle unaided in order to learn. Tell them the small signs of progress to look for so they can delight in being the first to see them.

Embarrassment

If your special child's problems are easily noticeable, you are aware of the difficulties you have when visiting strange places and meeting new people. I expect you are still sensitive to the reactions of strangers however much you have tried to grow a thicker skin.

In the same way, your other children may feel awkward and embarrassed when new friends realize their brother or sister is different. Help them to work out a simple explanation to give to friends, preferably one which includes what your special child can do and how other children can help. For example, 'Tony can't hear but he can understand what you are saying if you look directly at him and talk slowly and clearly'.

Life will be easier for your other children if their brother or sister is known and accepted in the community. One father took the brave step of talking at the school assembly when he found his children were being teased for having a severely handicapped brother. He spoke of his son's problems and how it must feel for him. Few people would have the courage to do that (I know I wouldn't) but the principle of meeting ignorance with information works.

Most children like to be the same as everyone else in their age group. This is especially important when they are in their teens, so your teenage children are particularly likely to be acutely embarrassed by their brother's or sister's strange appearance or behaviour. Although you can help in the ways I have already mentioned, you must accept their feelings. Try not to be hurt if they don't bring friends home and never force them to take your special child with them if they don't want to. That will only breed resentment.

Planning for the future

If your special child's difficulties are so great that he will never be fully independent, the question arises of what will happen to him when you are too old to cope anymore. It is unfair to assume that your other children will take on the caring role. They have their own lives to lead. Make sure they realize you do not expect them to take over from you in years to come.

If problems arise

Despite all your efforts, you may find that behaviour problems develop with your other children which you don't know how to handle. The earlier you ask for help the better. There is no shame in using child guidance, family therapy or whatever it is being called at the moment. You will probably feel awkward or embarrassed at the idea of one of your children seeing a psychiatrist, psychologist or psychotherapist but the service is there so why not use it? No one is suggesting your child is mad, just that he needs help to cope with his situation. It can be a great help to have someone you and your children can talk to who is outside the family and therefore not emotionally involved. Once you start to feel the benefits of some help, you will feel more relaxed about receiving it.

21

Grandparents

Your parents were probably some of the first people you turned to for support when you realized your child had problems. I hope you received the help you needed but you may have found them less supportive than you expected, especially in the early days.

After a lifetime of hard work and worry bringing up their own children, most people look forward to relaxing and enjoying their grandchildren. When their longed-for grandchild brings sorrow, as well as joy, their dreams are shattered. For your parents, your child's condition is a double tragedy. Although they grieve for their grandchild, they may be even sadder to see their own child (you) so hurt and unhappy.

The situation can be particularly difficult for a lone grandparent. He, or more probably she, has no one to turn to for support and no one with whom to share the worries or the sorrow. She may turn to you for the support she needs just when you have no energy spare to give it. If so, ask another relative or family friend to ease the demands on you by having more contact than usual with your Mum and Dad.

Early reactions

Being older than you, your parents were brought up at a time when handicap, especially mental handicap, was far less acceptable than it is today. They may never have known any handicapped people and their ideas may be influenced by old wives' tales and other misinformation. As a result they may take longer than you to accept what has happened.

Unlike you, they are not in the front line of child care so it is easier for them to opt out of the problem by opting out of contact with your child. Alternatively, they may try to deny the diagnosis, especially if your child appears normal. They may insist he is only a little slow not mentally handicapped or that his cystic fibrosis is only chestiness which he will outgrow. Worse still, they may insist his problems are all your fault – that all would be well if only you followed their advice.

All these reactions usually improve with time as your parents work through their grief; having trouble coping initially does not mean they will never be supportive. Give them as much information as you can about your child's problems and how they can be helped. Leaflets are particularly useful as your parents can read them many times, if necessary, rather than asking you to keep repeating facts and explanations. Remember they need to understand the situation before they can cope with it. Even if they opt out of visiting, continue to write or phone with news of their grandchild, stressing the positive side if you can.

If your parents hurt you by thoughtless comments or behaviour in those early weeks, try not to hold it against them for the rest of their lives. Even if the situation does not improve, try to feel sorrow at their inability to cope rather than anger at their reactions. Don't feel guilty either. If they cannot face what has happened, it is their problem not yours.

Why?

Grandmothers seem more worried than anyone else about 'Why it happened'. They are particularly prone to make comments like 'There's never been anything like that before in *our* side of the family'. Perhaps they feel an inner need to prove the situation is not their fault. This can be even more pronounced if your child's condition is inherited. Your Mum's comments then may blame your father's Uncle George who had a nasty cough or his Cousin Mildred who Mum always did think looked a little odd. . . . If all this talk of blame upsets you, try ignoring the comments so such conversations die in their early stages. If that fails, just state firmly 'I don't care where the problem came from so I would rather not discuss it' and stand by what you have said.

Grandparents can help

I am sure it eased your feelings of helplessness to know there were ways you could help your child. Similarly your parents may welcome suggestions on how to help you. Apart from obvious ideas like baby-sitting, they may enjoy practical tasks like altering clothes to fit your non-standard-shape child and making or adapting special toys or furniture.

Encourage both sets of grandparents to learn any special care skills or exercises your child needs so they feel confident enough to look after him themselves sometimes. As well as giving you a break, it will allow him to build the same close relationship with his grandparents that he would have had in the ordinary way.

Disagreements

Two major sources of friction between parents and grandparents are discipline and sweets. They tend to provide too little of the former and too many of the latter. Don't kid yourself that you have this problem because your child is handicapped or sick. It is universal to all families and you will probably be as bad yourself if you ever have grandchildren. On the other hand, your child's problems may heighten the tension if they mean that too little discipline or too many sweets are extra serious.

If your parents live a long way away so you only see them infrequently, you may find it best to grin and bear it while you are with them. Otherwise it is best to say how you feel early on and clear the air, rather than go on becoming more and more annoyed until you finally explode. It may be worth considering a compromise solution such as sweets once a week rather than no sweets at all. You could also suggest more acceptable treats such as favourite foods, comics or bubble liquid.

As time goes by

Supportive grandparents are worth their weight in gold but remember they are older than you. As time goes by, they will age and your child will grow taller and heavier. There may come a time when, however willing they are, they will not be able to give as much practical help as they did before. For that reason it is not a good idea to let them become your sole source of help.

As your parents become less able physically, suggest other ways they can help so they still feel useful. Elderly, retired grandparents may not be able to lift a heavy child on and off the toilet but they still have plenty of that valuable commodity, time: time to play a game over and over again, time to repeat exercises and time to listen. Together parents and grandparents can make a very good team.

22
Should we have Another Baby?

No one, least of all me, has the right to tell you and your partner how many children you should have. That decision is yours and yours alone.

It is easy for outsiders to understand your fears that your next baby will also have problems. To them, the obvious solution may be to avoid the risks and have no more children. Perhaps only other parents who have suffered the same heartaches can fully appreciate how much you may want another child even if the odds are stacked against you. Perhaps you feel a failure for producing an imperfect child so you want to try again to prove you can be like everyone else. Perhaps your special child is dying or already dead and you cannot bear to be left with empty arms. Perhaps you desperately want an ordinary child who can grow up, marry and give you grandchildren. All these feelings are natural and very common.

Finding out the facts

It is very important to make the right decision for you both, a decision you can bear to live with. The first step in making it is to ensure you have all the information you need. Probably you were told about any risk to further children when you were first given the diagnosis but the details may be a little fuzzy by now or completely forgotten. If you are unsure of the risks, ask your doctor to arrange for you to have genetic counselling. This may be given by your consultant or a specialist genetic counsellor and consists of a thorough explanation of the chances of your next child having similar problems to your previous one.

Feel free to ask as many questions as you like. The mechanics of inheritance are confusing to everyone when they meet them for the first time so no one will think you stupid for not understanding everything straight away. If possible, get a written explanation as well – perhaps the diagrams the doctor drew to illustrate her explanation or a leaflet from your voluntary society. It will jog your memory when you are talking things over at home or explaining the situation to relatives.

Pre-natal diagnosis

It may be possible for tests to be performed when you are pregnant to tell you if the new baby is affected or not. One common test involves taking a sample of the fluid surrounding the baby (amniocentesis) but new methods are constantly being developed. The range of conditions which can be detected before birth is also increasing all the time.

Your doctor may be unwilling to perform these tests if you only want them for your own peace of mind and definitely do not want a termination (abortion). In this case, ask to be referred to another doctor who would be willing to help.

If the tests show all is well you are spared months of worry but if they show the new baby has problems, you have the choice of continuing the pregnancy or having it terminated. If you find yourself in this situation, make sure you have all the facts about both alternatives before you make up your mind. Some parents feel they would be denying the worth of their special child if they terminated a pregnancy because the new baby had the same condition. That is obviously a very personal opinion but it is worth considering how you would explain a termination to your special child should he ever find out about it. Don't be pressurized into a decision which feels wrong – it is you who will have to live with its consequences, not the doctors. Deliberately becoming pregnant while relying on pre-natal diagnosis to ensure you have a healthy baby is not a decision to be taken lightly. The results of some pre-natal tests are not available until your pregnancy is well-advanced and a late termination will mean you have to undergo labour to deliver the baby. Also, although the idea of an abortion may seem acceptable beforehand, your views may change once you are pregnant. Some mothers find that, by the time the test results come, they are already too attached to the baby they are carrying to be able to agree to a termination.

If you have another baby

If you have another baby, you will probably be very anxious during the pregnancy even if the chances of the next baby being affected are very low. You have been unlucky once so you will never be completely confident again.

Once the baby is born, you may know straight away if all is well or you may have to await the results of tests or just watch anxiously for early symptoms. Whichever is the case think carefully before agreeing to stay in hospital for more than the minimum period unless it is essential for medical or practical reasons. However well-meaning the hospital staff are, they may not appreciate the depth of your anxieties and may assume all your emotions are merely 'baby-blues'. This is a time when you and your husband need to be together as much as possible to support each other.

Even if your new baby is perfectly all right, your joy may be tinged with sadness. Many mothers find that caring for a healthy baby and seeing it develop normally, reawakens their grief for their other child for it lets them see what might have been. You should find the sadness goes with time as you begin to appreciate your new child as a person in his or her own right.

Adoption

If you decide not to risk having another baby but still feel your family is incomplete, adoption may seem the ideal solution. It is no longer as easy to adopt a young baby as it was years ago. Better contraception and easily available abortion have combined with a greater acceptance of a single parenthood to drastically reduce the number of babies available for adoption. Demand now exceeds supply, so social workers can be very selective when choosing which couples to use as adoptive parents.

Nevertheless, there are still children needing homes. If either or both of you are Black or of mixed race, you will find social workers keen to consider you as adoptive parents. They like to place children in homes of similar racial background to their own and there are sometimes more Black or mixed race children waiting than there are homes available.

The other children needing homes are the hard-to-place ones. Some are handicapped, some are well past babyhood and others are in family groups of two or more brothers or sisters who wish to stay together. Social workers find it more difficult to find new parents for these children so are more open-minded when assessing prospective adopters. In particular, they relax the strict age rules usually applied to baby adoption.

Some of the children have difficult backgrounds involving many changes of home, neglect or physical or sexual abuse. Taking such a child into your home is a big step which must not be taken lightly. To

103

work with a damaged child and see him or her blossom into a happy, confident member of your family is very satisfying but enormously hard work. It may mean persisting for months or years with little sign of progress or allowing an older child to regress back to babyhood for a while. You need plenty of patience and a good sense of humour.

If you are interested in adoption, you can obtain further information from PPIAS or you can contact your local social services department or an adoption agency. Some social workers may reject your application because you have a sick or handicapped child in your family. This may be because of their own personal bias so, if it happens to you, try another agency.

Fostering

Some children need permanent homes but also wish to remain in contact with their original families. Others need to stay somewhere for a few days, weeks or months but will eventually either return home or move to a permanent new family. Both these groups of children need foster care.

Fostering means taking a child into your family but sharing him with his natural parents. It means loving a child and letting him go again. Short-term fostering, in particular, means never being quite sure how many children you will have next month or next year. Keeping in touch with natural parents involves welcoming people into your house who you might never have chosen as friends, people who may be feeling vulnerable and unhappy.

To foster successfully you need more than a desire for another child. It helps to have a sense of humour, patience, time and a non-judgemental view of other people. Don't let me put you off too much though – you don't need to be a saint! Fostering can be fun and brings its own rewards. We have done it for several years and never regretted it. Your local social services department can tell you more about fostering (ask to speak to the fostering and adoption officer) or you can contact the National Fostercare Association.

PART FIVE
Death and Dying

23

If your Child might Die

Not all children with special needs die young. Many have a normal life expectancy. However, the sad truth is that some special children are extra vulnerable to infections while others have terminal illnesses. If you know your child may or definitely will die, you have every right to feel frightened. For you, every parent's nightmare is a reality.

When our boys were first diagnosed, the prognosis for cystic fibrosis was much worse than it is today so the fear of losing them was very real. It haunted me. I dreamt I was at their funerals. When other parents talked of choosing primary schools, we wondered if they would live long enough ever to go to school. Occasionally we would hear of another CF child who had died and our blood would run cold. I would hold my baby close, trying to protect him from these dangers I did not fully understand.

So how can you live with the prospect of approaching death, whether it is a certainty or just a possibility? There is no one way of coping. I cannot give you the perfect solution for everyone is different. I can only suggest ideas based on my own experiences and those of other parents and the professionals who work with them.

Try, if you can, to look your fear in the face and admit it is there. Talk to each other about it. Ask the doctors what is likely to happen. How rapidly will the disease progress? Is death likely to come suddenly without warning or will it be preceded by a gradual deterioration? Such questions may sound morbid but it is easier to face something if you know as much about it as possible.

If death is still a long way off or only a possibility, you have to try to move on, to return to the world of the living. Although you know what the future could bring, you need to push that knowledge to one side and live for today, not thinking too far ahead. It is a mental trick you can acquire with practice but you won't manage it all the time. Occasionally some event or chance phrase will trigger all your emotions again and you will feel in turmoil. Accept the feelings as natural, don't make yourself feel even worse by feeling guilty about them.

If the prospect of death is more imminent, you have to cope with the realities of the situation. There are practical decisions to make but remember there are no right or wrong answers. Every child and every family is different. Listen to the advice offered but don't let people talk you into actions which feel wrong. Make the decisions which feel right for you and your family for it is you who will have to live with them.

Brothers and sisters

It is frightening to be part of a family where something is wrong but you do not know what it is. It can leave a child isolated and alone. My father died of cancer when I was 14 and I was trapped by the secrecy which surrounded the disease at that time. No one spoke to me about what was happening, I did not feel able to talk about it either. Years later I can still remember my loneliness.

Don't exclude your other children from what is happening. Give them a chance to talk about their fears. They need to know you still love them, that they still matter, even though their brother or sister takes so much of your time. If you find it difficult to give them as much attention as they need, perhaps a relative or close friend could spend extra time with them.

Try to involve your other children as much as you can. If your sick child is at home, show them ways to help if they want to – perhaps they could work the tape recorder, play games or read stories. If their brother or sister is in hospital, encourage them to visit, draw pictures and write letters. Don't expect them to be miserable all the time. Let them laugh and play as much as they want. Your sick child will probably enjoy life going on around him.

If you spoil your dying child, you may breed resentment in your other children. Remember you don't have to shower a child with material things to show him you love him. Giving him time and attention does that. Of course, there may be special places you want to visit and things you want to do before it is too late but those treats do not have to be exclusively for your sick child. If possible, make them family events for you all to share and for you all to remember.

Sharing with your dying child

The issue of how much to tell your child about his illness is a very emotive one. There are no certain rules to follow for all children are different. I am grateful to Lenore Hill for allowing me to quote the following advice she gave in an article for parents. She is currently

Head Nurse at Martin House so she has worked with many dying children and their families.

Some children remain very aware of the treatment that they are going through and of the life they are living. Others have become less aware because of the nature of the disease, but for children who are aware and able to understand, it is important that you share with them as you share with the brothers and sisters, but *you* will know what is right to do for *your* family. You will be sensitive to your own children, and to the questions they are asking. It is important to go at the child's pace and not to rush in there in front with things they haven't got round to asking about yet. But as they do ask it is important to be able to spend time with them and to be able to answer their questions honestly. Some parents find this very difficult, especially if the child is going to die. But I think that if we are not honest with them, if we don't share with them, it doesn't actually protect them. There are very few children who are not conscious of the truth. What we do is isolate them in the situation by themselves, because they will try to protect you. If they put out feelers and you don't answer they will withdraw, they'll realise that it's too hurtful for you, and they will stop asking, but they won't be unaware. They'll just be isolated in their situation, because you've not let them talk to you.

All I would add is that if you really cannot meet your child's need to talk about the prospect of his death, try to find someone else who can. It could be a close friend, a grandparent, a nurse, a psychotherapist or anyone else your child trusts. Qualifications are less important than personality.

Easing the strain

Caring for a child with a life-threatening progressive disorder is hard work, physically and emotionally. A very special type of help is available from Martin House and Helen House (sometimes called children's hospices). They offer long-term friendship and support to your entire family. You can all stay for a while or you can leave your child there while you have a holiday, give the other children extra attention or catch up on the chores and your sleep.

Once you are in touch with them, their support is available

throughout your child's illness. It does not even stop when he dies but continues afterwards to help you through your grief. If you feel one of the Houses could help you, ask your doctor or another professional to make enquiries or you can contact them yourself. At the time of writing, there are plans for more such Houses in other parts of the country – your doctor should know about any new ones.

Facing the inevitable

Obviously the doctors will do as much for your child as they can. With many conditions, they will keep fighting death until the very end. Sometimes though, a time comes when no amount of treatment will prevent the inevitable, when the extra few days which may be won by yet another course of drugs is not enough to justify putting your child through yet more unpleasant side-effects.

Once again there are no hard and fast rules. Be sensitive to your child's feelings and, if you think both you and he have had enough, talk to the doctors. Perhaps the time has come to limit treatment to making your child as comfortable as possible.

Where?

If death comes suddenly, you will have no say in where it happens. However, if your child is slowly deteriorating, the question arises of where he should be at the end. Once again there is no right answer. What is right for you depends on your own feelings and your child's, how much you feel you can cope with and what support you have. If you have good medical care available at home through visiting doctors and nurses, you may feel more able to cope at home than you could with no help available. If you are already in touch with Helen House or Martin House, you may feel that is the best place for your child to die.

Do what feels right for you as a family, whatever anyone else says. In particular, don't feel you have failed your child if you decide initially he should spend his last days at home but unforeseen circumstances force his admission to hospital at the last minute.

Practicalities

Immediately after your child dies, you will be faced with some decisions which have to be made quickly just as you feel too upset to

110

decide anything. If you can force yourself to think about them in advance, you may save yourself making decisions in the heat of the moment which you later regret.

After death, your child will be washed and dressed. If you would like to do this yourselves as part of the process of saying goodbye, say so in advance to the nurses caring for your child. Otherwise they may not think to ask if you want to help when the time arises. As with everything else, there is no right way to behave. Only do this if you want to – you will not be letting your child down if you don't.

Post-mortems

In those first hours after your child's death, it can hurt to be asked for permission for a post-mortem. If you have already seen your child suffer many painful treatments, it is easy to turn down the idea, feeling he should now be left in peace. However, you may regret the decision later if the exact nature of your child's condition is not known. A post-mortem may be the only hope you have for a proper diagnosis to tell you the risks to any future children although it is fair to point out that it may not provide the answers you need. If you can face up to the prospect, discuss the idea of a post-mortem with your child's doctors before he dies when it may be easier to listen objectively to the arguments.

Organ donation

Another idea worth discussing in advance with the doctors is the possibility of donating any of your child's organs for transplantation. At the time of death you may be too upset to ask about it and others may hesitate to broach the subject for fear of upsetting you further. By the time you think of the possibility, it may be too late.

Some parents feel their child has already gone through too much and should be left in peace. Others feel helped by knowing their own child's death has, at least, saved another family from the sorrow they themselves face. An older child may have indicated his own feelings on this issue, perhaps by carrying a donor card. Please don't be disappointed if your offer for your child's organs to be used is rejected. His illness may mean they are not suitable.

111

Funerals

Arranging the funeral requires a whole flood of decisions. Should it be a burial or cremation? Should you ask for flowers or donations to charity? Do you want a religious service? Which music do you want? It may seem morbid to consider these questions before your child dies but to do so can ease the load later. One family even went to the trouble of visiting all the undertakers long before their child's death and choosing which they would use. They then felt able to relax, knowing that when the time came they could put the arrangements in the hands of someone they trusted.

I doubt if many people could go this far but it is sensible to think of the other issues. An older child may express his own preference on burial or cremation. Otherwise choose what feels right to you. Some people like to have a grave to give them a place to visit; others don't.

You don't have to have a religious service at a funeral unless you want one. Some people design their own ceremony, playing favourite music and asking friends to read words with particular meaning to the family. If you have no religious connections but want a service, you can avoid the impersonality which can result from the priest being a stranger by asking him to read out something written by the family about your childs' life.

Remember, above all, that funerals are for the living, they are part of the grieving process. By then your child will be free like a butterfly. All you are disposing of is the cocoon, the discarded shell.

24
Talking to Children about Death

Death has replaced sex as the great taboo in our society. Children are protected from it. It is spoken about in hushed voices and forgotten as soon as possible.

If a child faces the possibility of the early death of himself or of one of his brothers and sisters, the often used explanation, 'People die when they get very old', is not enough. It is difficult, though, to talk easily about such a potentially painful subject. Perhaps we need to feel comfortable with our own feelings before we can share them with others.

Death is a natural part of life. We are all working towards it from the moment of birth. Personally, I believe it is a transition, the next step. Only the smallness of our minds makes us see it as failure or disaster. Something goes at death – the life force, the spirit, the soul. Call it what you will, it is gone. What is left behind is the empty shell like the cocoon after the butterfly has flown.

I do not know where that spirit goes – no one does for sure. Personally, I believe it moves on to somewhere better. Many people who have died but been resuscitated, speak of a reluctance to return, of seeing lost relatives again and feeling surrounded by love. Stories abound of people smiling at the moment of death or speaking of seeing a light.

What happens to people when they die?

When children ask what happens when you die, there is nothing wrong in admitting you do not know. If you feel comfortable doing so, you can talk about your own beliefs and/or those of other people. You might want to mention some of the ideas in the last section. Be sensitive to their questions so you proceed at their pace, neither holding back what they need to know nor rushing ahead into topics they are not ready for yet.

Your child may want to talk about what life after death might be like. In particular, he may like the idea of leaving physical problems behind on earth, of there being no muscular dystrophy, cystic fibrosis or cancer in heaven. However, even the most wonderful after-life can sound frighteningly lonely without Mum and Dad. Remembering people you know who have already died and Jesus (if you are Christians) can help both your sick child and his brothers and sisters to feel someone will be there to care about him.

'If you are good, you'll go to heaven' is an idea many children hear but, of course, no child is ever completely good. Yours may need reassurance that whatever happens after death is dependent on God and his love rather than on whether your child wrote on the wall in felt-tip pen.

Is death frightening?

By protecting children from the facts of death, we can easily give the impression death is very frightening. Why else would we hide it? Why else would we not take them to Great Grandma's funeral?

Our children see death every day on TV. The news shows violence and destruction, both natural and man-made. Actors depict death from a multitude of sources – guns, poison, arrows and accident. The only type of death rarely shown is the natural one occurring peacefully in bed. It is easy for young children to assume all death is violent, that the trickle of blood from the actor's mouth is natural rather than added for dramatic effect.

When talking to your children about death, make it clear the image on TV is a distorted one. Although it may be preceded by pain and illness, death itself is not terrible for the one who dies. It is a step into the unknown but not frightening in itself. We cry about it because of our own pain, our own loss and our own loneliness.

25

Death and Bereavement

If your child dies after a long illness, your first reaction may well be relief. Your child will suffer no longer and the enormous burden of care you have born is finally lifted. Far from being unable to sleep with grief as friends expect, you may sleep better the first night than for many weeks. For the first time you do not have to listen for your child so you can start to overcome the sheer exhaustion which has developed during the previous weeks.

If you react like this you are not being heartless. The tears and grief will come eventually, hours, days or even weeks later. Don't feel guilty about your relief. It is only natural. There is no right or wrong way to react to this death. Your emotions are beyond your control – accept how you feel as being right for you at this point of time.

The funeral

Funerals are for the living not the dead. They are part of the grieving process, forcing those left behind to accept the reality of what has happened and providing an opportunity for them to share their grief openly.

If losing your child is the first time you have encountered a close death, you may have never attended a funeral before. Most people are frightened the first time they go to one so don't worry if you are too. However, don't back out of attending through fear of the unknown, you will probably regret it later and there is no second chance.

Funerals are very, very, sad but not frightening. If you are worried, ask the undertaker, the priest, a friend or relative to explain exactly what will happen. In particular, ask what happens to the coffin during a cremation if that is worrying you. The answer varies from one place to another. Sometimes it will be lowered out of sight or slide out through doors in a side wall. Alternatively curtains or gates may close, separating that part of the chapel from the congregation. Whatever happens is symbolic, you don't see the actual cremation.

People have mixed feelings about children attending funerals.

Personally, I believe that children who are aware of the death of their brother or sister should be encouraged to attend the funeral. Of course, they may be frightened of the idea so either you or someone else they trust should explain what will happen and try to calm the fears, reassuring them that no one will mind whether they cry or not. If you think you will be too upset to support your other children through the service, ask a close friend or relative to do this for you.

Before the funeral

For many parents, seeing their child's body helps them accept the reality of death. If you were with your child when he died, you will do this automatically. It will probably feel natural to hold him and say goodbye. If you were not with him, you will be able to choose whether to see him or not. This decision is a very personal one and there is no right or wrong choice. If you are in doubt, remember it is better to go sooner rather than later. Your child will look far more dead after three or four days than he will in the first few hours.

Your other children may wish to see their brother or sister. They can be helped by this to realize that all that is left behind is a shell, an empty house. The living being who they laughed and played and fought with is not there anymore. Let them visit if they wish but don't force them if they don't want to go.

It is up to you how involved you are in the arrangements – again, do what feels comfortable to you. You may want to choose the clothes your child wears and perhaps also dress him and (if he is small enough) place him in the coffin yourself. You and your other children may wish to place special toys or letters in the coffin with him. (These can be removed just before the funeral if you want to keep them.) Some parents choose to carry their baby's coffin themselves. All these are right to do if they help you but it is equally right not to do them if you don't want to.

Possessions

If your child was old enough to realize he was dying, he may have said what he wanted to happen to his things. Otherwise the decisions are yours. Don't forget you are not the only people grieving. Your child's school friends and brothers and sisters may like to be offered something tangible to remember him by. Don't

116

feel you have to get rid of everything. Some parents pack away items they cannot face until they are more accustomed to their grief.

If you have lost a baby and plan to have more children, you may want to keep the baby clothes and equipment for your next child. Some people cannot face this, prefering to start afresh next time while others compromise by keeping the major items of equipment but disposing of the clothes. Once again there is no right way of behaving.

Grief

However much you were expecting the death, the loss of your child will turn your whole world upside down. Nothing will ever be the same again and, in that sense, it is true to say you will never get over it. You will, however, become used to it in time. There will be happy times again although you will never forget this child you have lost.

If you have never previously lost anyone close to you, the intensity of your grief may be frightening. You may fear you are losing your mind but you are not. Grief is a natural process to be worked through however painful it may feel at the time. Tranquillizers and sleeping pills are not the answer. They may make it easier for those around you to cope by making your reactions less intense but for you they only delay your mourning, they don't replace it.

At first, you may feel numb, unable to accept what has happened and react to it. Long established habits cannot be unlearned in an instant, so don't be surprised if you still lay the extra place for meals, buy enough food for your lost child or even buy clothes for him. Other parents find the same problems. You will also not be alone if you make silly mistakes and find it difficult to perform simple tasks and easy household jobs. One mother told me how, shortly after her son's death, she unloaded the frozen food from her shopping and put it in the oven instead of the freezer.

As the numbness wears off, other emotions surface. As well as sadness, depression and loneliness, you may feel anger, resentment and guilt. These emotions don't come tidily in order. You can't think 'Oh, good, I'm at the angry stage so I only have resentment and guilt left to work through'. Instead they come jumbled up so you jump from one to the other, sometimes at bewildering speed.

You may also suffer physical symptoms of distress – loss of appetite, indigestion or headaches to name but a few. You may find you can't concentrate, that you panic more easily and that you worry more about the safety and well-being of the other people you love. All these reactions are as natural as the tears everyone expects from you.

Grief is an individual process. You, your partner and your other children may all react differently, experiencing the various emotions at different times. Anger over the death may spill out in the form of short temper and petty rows. Your children may be clingy, demanding or bad tempered just as neither of you feel able to cope with them. Hang on – don't give up. Stay together and keep talking for life will slowly return to a new normality.

Brothers and sisters

Your other children will need to grieve for their dead brother or sister. Don't pour all your energy into keeping life going on normally or you may make them think they should hide their feelings. Just as you find it difficult at first to cope with everyday life, they may need a short break from school before they can cope again. It gives them time to share in what is going on and to cry with you.

If your other children are very young, they may keep expecting their brother or sister to come back as they do not understand the finality of death. Only time will help them learn the truth and their grief may be reawakened when they do.

Your other children probably did not like their dead brother or sister all the time. They may have shouted at him, told him to go away or secretly wished he was dead so they could have all the attention he was receiving from you. This can leave them full of guilt once their brother or sister has died. They may even worry that they caused the death by wishing for it and need reassurance that none of what has happened was their fault.

Other people

Some people may avoid you after your child's death because they don't know what to say. Others feel they must say something and come out with platitudes that hurt. 'It's a release' and 'It's better this way' can make you feel guilty for grieving, as if your hurt should be less because your child had special needs. Worse still are the comments like 'You're young enough to have another baby' which suggest children are replaceable like toy dolls.

People are not trying to hurt you – they are just trying to help but being very misguided in the attempt. Perhaps there are no right words beyond the simple expressions of sorrow and sympathy.

The friends who can help are those who can listen to your feelings without judging you and talk with you about your lost child without embarrassment at your tears. One home teacher for pre-school children told me how she always continues going to the home after a child has died until the mother herself feels ready for the visits to stop. She drinks tea and shares memories, talking about the child and looking at photos, for she realizes how much bereaved parents need to talk about their dead child and how difficult it is for them to do it. Many parents complain of a conspiracy of silence among the people they meet who all avoid any mention of their child.

Many parents find support from others who have lost children. From them, they gain reassurance that their reactions are not abnormal. With them, they find understanding of their needs to talk about their child. If you feel you would benefit from such support, contact The Compassionate Friends who can put you in touch with other bereaved parents willing to help you.

Avoid big decisions

It is easy to want to run away from all the hurtful memories, to move to a new house and new surroundings. However, the early stages of grief are not the times to make such important decisions. You are not yourselves and you can easily make changes you will later regret. A move now may lose the painful memories but it will also lose the good ones and your friends. Your other children too have enough to handle without expecting them to cope with changing schools.

It is also better not to rush into having another baby. Wait until you are more accustomed to your grief so you can accept your new child as an individual rather than as a replacement for the one you have lost.

Keep busy

Other bereaved parents have all recommended keeping busy. Dad probably is anyway unless he gave up work to help care for his child.

It is usually Mum who finds the hours endless while everyone is out all day. Find something to fill those empty hours – a job, voluntary work, redecorating, anything which will force you to keep busy.

In the long term

Be prepared for grief lasting a long time. Other people may expect you back to normal in a few weeks but you won't be. Readjustment to this new reality takes months not days. You will never forget this child you have lost but you will learn to live with your memories, to feel joy and happiness again. That does not mean the old ache will not return on his birthday or when you realize that he would now be starting school. But you can move on to a new life, hopefully better people for having had this child, however briefly.

While I have been researching, many people have shared with me words which have brought them comfort. I have not room to include them all but I am ending this section with the one I find most helpful myself.

Death is nothing at all. I have only slipped away into the next room. I am I and you are you. Whatever we were to each other we still are. Call me by my old familiar name, speak to me in the easy way which you always used. Put no difference in your tone, wear no forced air of solemnity and sorrow. Laugh as we always laughed at the little jokes we enjoyed together. Pray, smile, think of me, pray for me. Let my name be always the household word that it always was, let it be spoken without effect, without the trace of a shadow in it. Life means all that it ever meant. It is the same as it ever was; there is unbroken continuity. Why should I be out of mind because I am out of sight? I am waiting for you, for an interval, somewhere very near, just around the corner. All is well.

Henry Scott Holland (1847–1918) Canon of St Paul's Cathedral

PART SIX
Growing Up

26

Special School or Ordinary School?

Years ago education for children with special needs was poor or non-existent. Some children were classified as ineducable, others were sent to special schools with problems which would today seem quite minor.

Over the years, the situation has gradually improved. No parent now receives a letter declaring their child to be 'unsuitable for education in school'. Children are no longer rigidly classified into delicate, blind, severely subnormal and all the other categories which existed. The 1981 Education Act changed the system so that the special educational needs of each child are now individually assessed to ensure he or she receives the most appropriate education. The Act also enshrines the idea that all children should attend ordinary school wherever possible (a principle often called integration). However, this does not mean special schools have ceased to exist nor are they likely to do so in the near future. For some children they are still the right placement.

Special schools

On the plus side, a special school will offer small classes in suitable buildings with teachers who have usually had some special training. The staff will be aware of the difficulties you face and special schools often have good links to the support services. Physiotherapy and occuptional therapy are usually available at school and there should be no problems about administering drugs. Your child will meet other children like him which will help to prevent him feeling isolated by his problems.

However, unless you are very lucky, the school is likely to be a long way away necessitating a long daily journey or boarding education. As a result, your child will lack local friends and you will have only limited contact with other parents as you will not meet them in the playground. Special schools, especially residential ones, offer a sheltered environment which does not prepare your child for the rough and tumble of normal life. Some schools (but not all) offer only a limited range of subjects and their pupils lack the opportunity to take exams, although the introduction of the National

Curriculum may change this. Parents also complain that children at special schools lack normal children to copy and may pick up strange behaviour and mannerisms from more severely handicapped children.

Ordinary schools

Education at an ordinary school offers plenty of contact with ordinary children. The school will probably be local so both you and your child will gain from a network of friends and acquaintances. However, your child may feel isolated if he is the only child with problems and some parents find the other children and the staff are over-protective. One mother described her son (who has Down's Syndrome) being dressed in his coat and gloves by two adoring little girls when he was quite capable of doing it by himself.

Ordinary school offers the full range of subjects and the opportunity to take exams. However, it will have larger classes and teachers untrained in special teaching methods. Sometimes a special assistant in the classroom can ease these problems. The buildings may also present practical difficulties which will have to be overcome.

Finding the right solution

Try to forget all the generalized arguments about integration. The most important thing for your child is that he goes to the right school for him: the one where he can be happy, receive all the help he needs and achieve his full potential. Whether that means an ordinary or a special school will depend not only on his problems but on his personality and on the schools available. Also the right solution now may not remain the right one as he grows older and his needs change. Let's consider some hypothetical children to show you what I mean.

James has Down's Syndrome and spent his pre-school years attending the local playschool. He mixed well and made local friends. However, by the time he was five the gap between him and his friends was growing, especially in language, and his parents could see that he needed more specialized help than he would receive at the ordinary school. He now attends the local special school where he enjoys being one of the best pupils, but he also spends two afternoons a week at the local primary school where he benefits from contact with ordinary children.

Laura appears completely normal but had not learned to speak by the time she was due to start school. As she was obviously unable to benefit from mainstream education, she attended a special school for children with speech and language disorders. Intensive speech therapy gave her the help she needed so that when she was ten she spoke well enough to transfer to an ordinary school.

Patricia's eyesight is very poor which makes reading and writing difficult. She coped well at primary school where the teachers understood her problems and her special assistant gave her as much help as she needed. However, when she changed to secondary school the different teaching techniques caused problems. Each subject had a different teacher and they did not all remember Patricia's needs. Teachers now wrote rapidly on the board in small writing instead of in the large round script of the primary school. Patricia started to slip behind in her work and became increasingly discouraged until she stopped trying. A transfer to a school for the visually handicapped restored her lost confidence so she was able to gain good exam results and go on to higher education.

Tracy has temporal lobe epilepsy which causes periods of difficult behaviour. The ordinary school she attended was unhelpful, insisting on disciplining her even though the reasons for her behaviour were known. Tracy became unhappy and lost all her confidence, assuming no one would like her and she would never be good at anything. The school recommended transfer to a special school but the LEA agreed to try her first at a different primary school with an ancillary helper to occupy her when she lost concentration. The new arrangements proved so successful that Tracy rapidly regained her self-confidence and became enthusiastic about school.

Choosing a school

Before you can decide what is right for your child, you need to know the alternatives. Visit all the available schools, including the special ones and the ordinary schools which are further afield. Read each school's brochure carefully and ask around among other parents as well, to get a consumer's eye view.

Try to make an appointment to visit a school during school hours so you can see it functioning. Talk to the headteacher and, if possible, to the person who would teach your child or be responsible for him (perhaps the head of year or special-needs coordinator). It is important to try to find out how the staff will react to your child and his problems as that can make such a difference to his happiness.

If you are visiting a special school, find out how your child will fit in with the other children. Are they noticeably more or less handicapped than he is? How good an education will he receive? Will he be taught the full National Curriculum and will he be able to take any exams? How well will his education prepare him for adult life? A good way to assess the replies to the last question is to ask what happens to other children when they leave.

When visiting ordinary schools, talk to the staff as well as looking at the suitability of the buildings. Will they make such heavy weather of your child's problems that he will feel different and miserable? Will he be able to take part in most of the normal activities or will he have to do different things most of the time? How do the staff feel about administering drugs or taking him on school outings? Are they so concerned that they will swamp him with help, so preventing him developing independence? I am not suggesting all of these problems will arise, just that they are worth considering.

Choosing a school is a difficult task. The world is an imperfect place so there may be no perfect solution to your child's education needs. For example, the ideal school may exist but be so far away he would have to be a boarder. In the end you may have to settle for the best possible compromise, but whichever school you choose, your support and encouragement will be vital ingredients in your child's success there.

27

Assessments and Statements

The 1981 Education Act declared that if a child has special educational needs, these should be assessed carefully before plans for his or her education are decided. The results of this assessment are written down in a document called a 'Statement of Special Educational Needs' which also includes the Local Education Authority's proposals to meet those needs. The LEA is then legally obliged to follow those plans.

Your child does not automatically need an assessment just because he has more problems than other children. His difficulties may not affect his education at all or the school may be managing to meet his needs anyway. An assessment is necessary if your child needs extra or additional help to that normally available at school – for example, if he needs extra practical support, special equipment or specialized teaching methods. In particular, he should have a statement if he attends a special unit attached to an ordinary school or a special school.

If your child is going to be assessed or you think he should be, find out about the process beforehand. This is particularly important if you think you are likely to disagree with the LEA's plans. When the LEA informs you of their intention to assess your child, they should also tell you about the procedures involved and about your rights as parents as well as giving you the name of an official whom you can contact for further information. Don't hesitate to ask questions about anything which is unclear or to ask other organisations for information. Personally, I have always found the Advisory Centre for Education very helpful with individual queries and they publish *The ACE Special Education Handbook*, an excellent guide to assessment which includes specimen letters to help you when writing to the LEA. Network '81 or your voluntary society may also be able to give you useful information and advice.

Either the school, another LEA official or yourselves as parents can ask for the assessment to be done. If the LEA decide to assess your child but you do not think it is necessary or are uncertain about it, write and say so, giving your reasons. Your arguments will sound stronger if you have the support of someone official who knows your child (a teacher, doctor or social worker, for example). Make sure your letter arrives before the time limit stated in the notification from the authority.

The method of assessment is laid down in the Act and includes medical, psychological and school reports plus an opportunity for you to state your views. In fact, one of the best things about the procedure is the way it forces communication between all concerned. The whole process can take a long time. There is no harm in phoning occasionally to ask how it is progressing – it may remind someone to chase a missing report.

The opportunity to express your views is a valuable one, so make the most of it. You have years of knowledge about your child which can be valuable to those planning for his future but it can be difficult deciding which information to include. Professor Sheila Wolfendale, an educational psychologist, with others, developed and produced Guidelines to help parents write their contribution to the assessment. With her permission, I have included a copy of them at the end of this chapter.

After the assessment

Before the Statement is made, the authority should send you a draft copy of it together with copies of all the reports written by the professionals involved. Read them all carefully, even if you agree with the LEA's plans, as you don't want any mistakes (however small) recorded for posterity. Make sure the Statement contains precise indications of need rather than vague comments. For example, 'some speech therapy' is less acceptable than 'speech therapy twice a week'.

Although you have a right to state your views you do not have a right of veto if you do not like the authority's plans. However, you are allowed to comment on the draft statement and, if you still disagree with the final one, you have a right of appeal. If you find yourself battling with an uncooperative LEA, it is particularly important to know your rights. You may find your voluntary society, Network '81 or ACE very helpful and *The ACE Special Education Handbook* could be invaluable. You could also try the Independent Panel of Special Education Experts if you feel an independent assessment might be useful.

If you are telling the LEA that you disagree with the draft statement, make your reasons clear. Perhaps you feel some of the reports are inaccurate or you cannot understand them. Perhaps you agree with the reports but feel the description of your child's special needs has not taken them all into account. Maybe the special educational and/or non-educational provision the LEA propose is inadequate or rather vague, or the school is not the one you wanted.

Don't just disagree – try to suggest some viable alternatives: ways the Statement could be changed so you would agree with it. You may like to ask for support from one or more of the professionals who know your child or from the school you would like your child to attend. You could also obtain an alternative assessment of your child from someone independent of the authority.

The National Curriculum

As I write this, the National Curriculum is only just coming into force so no one can yet see how it will work in practice. Obviously, some children will not be able to cope with the National Curriculum so there is provision in the legislation for children to be excluded from all or part of it and for the Curriculum to be modified. If anyone suggests this for your child, ask why they feel this is a good idea and what he will be taught instead.

If your child has a statement, any necessary changes to the effect of the National Curriculum will be stated in the section on 'special educational provision'. This will be included when a new Statement is written or if the existing Statement is amended. In either case, you have a right of appeal if you do not agree with the plans. If no change is suggested but you feel it may be necessary, first talk to the school about your concerns. Then, if necessary, ask the authority to reassess your child.

If your child has no statement, he may be temporarily excluded from all or part of the National Curriculum on the decision of his head teacher. If you are worried about any aspect of the way the Curriculum is being applied to your child, talk to the head about it. If you are still not happy you can appeal to the governors. Then, if you are still not satisfied, you can complain through the LEA curriculum complaints procedure.

Guidelines for Parents Contributing to an Assessment

Introduction

These guidelines are to help you with your contribution to the assessment. You do not have to use them if you do not want to, you may change the order, leave bits out or add things you may feel to be important. It would be useful, however, if you used the headings we have suggested. Your written contribution may be as short or as long as you wish.

A - The Early Years

1. What do you remember about the early years that might help?
2. What was (*name*) like as a young baby?
3. Were you happy at the time with his progress?
4. When did you first feel things were not right?
5. What happened?
6. Did you receive any advice or help – from whom?

B – What is Your Child Like Now?

1 General health

Eating and sleeping habits; general fitness, absences from school; minor ailments – coughs and colds. Serious illnesses/accidents; periods in hospital. Any medicine or special diet?

Also for older children: general alertness, tiredness; signs of use of drugs – smoking, drinking, glue-sniffing.

2 Physical skills

Younger children: Crawling, walking, jumping, running, climbing stairs; catching, building bricks, doing jigsaws; scribbling, drawing, writing; sewing.

Older children: Walking, running, climbing, riding a bike, football or other games; drawing pictures, writing, doing jigsaws; using construction kits, household gadgets, tools, sewing.

3 Self-help

Younger children: Dressing, undressing; feeding, eating; toileting; brushing, combing hair, washing hands and face, wiping nose, etc.

Older children: Level of personal independence – dressing, etc; making bed, washing clothes, keeping room tidy, coping with day-to-day routine; budgeting pocket money; general independence – getting out and about.

4 Communication

Younger children: Points, makes gestures; copies sounds; uses single words, phrases, sentences; understands and responds to others, starts conversations, chats, describes events, people.

Older children: Level of speech – explains, describes events, people; conveys information (e.g., messages to and from school), joins in conversations; uses telephone.

5 Playing and learning at home

Younger children: Favourite toys and activities, concentration; playing alone, sharing games, stories, etc; watching television.

Older children: How (name) spends time – watching TV, reading for pleasure and information, hobbies; concentration; sharing.

6 Activities outside

Younger children: Attendance at playgroup, nursery, etc; coping with separation for short/long periods.

Older children: Belonging to clubs, sporting activities, happy to go alone.

7 Relationships

With parents, brothers and sisters; with friends; with other adults (friends and relations) at home generally, 'outside' generally.
Is (name) a loner?

8 Behaviour at home

Co-operates, shares, listens to and carries out requests, helps in the house, offers help, fits in with family routine and 'rules'. Moods good and bad, sulking – temper tantrums; demonstrative, affectionate.

9 At school

Relationships with other children and teachers; progress with reading, writing, numbers, other subjects and activities at school. How the school has helped/not helped with your child. Have you been asked to help with school work – hearing child read – with what result?
Does (name) enjoy school?
What does (name) find easy or difficult?

C – *Your General Views*

1. How do you compare your child with others of the same age?
2. What is your child good at or enjoys doing?
3. What does (*name*) worry about – is (*name*) aware of difficulties?
4. What are your worries, concerns?
5. Is there any other information you would like to give:
   (a) about the family – major events which may have affected your child?
   (b) reports from other people?
6. What do you think your child's special needs are?
7. How do you think these can best be provided for?
8. With whom would you like more contact?
9. What do you think are your family's needs and your needs?

Sheila Wolfendale *The Parental Contribution to Assessment* (1988)
National Council for Special Education

28
Getting the Best from School

Good communication lies at the heart of a good relationship between you and the school. If the staff do not understand your child's special needs, they will not be able to meet them properly. If you do not understand what the school are trying to achieve, you will be unable to support those aims at home.

Most schools rely on notes and word of mouth to carry information back and forth between home and school. Some children, mine included, are dreadful at delivering letters and the situation is even more difficult if your child cannot speak. One solution used by some schools (including my son's) is to always send letters home on the same day each week so parents know when to search the school bag. Some special schools use another technique involving a book where parents and teachers can write notes on what has happened at school and home. The book goes back and forth with the child each day and is particularly valuable for non-speaking children. You could suggest either of these ideas to your school if you find communications a problem.

Basic information

Before your child starts a new school, talk to the staff about his special needs. This is particularly important if the school have never had a child like yours before. Make an appointment to see the relevant teachers rather than trying to talk at an ordinary parents' evening when everyone will feel rushed.

You need to be very specific about any special care your child needs. Try not to alarm and frighten the teachers who may already be feeling apprehensive about this new pupil, especially if they have not previously taught a child who has his particular difficulties. Teachers can feel very inadequate when faced with a potentially vulnerable child and ignorance can cause them to be over-protective. Comments like 'I don't like to push him as I know he's ill' and 'I didn't realize I could take her out of her wheelchair' are infuriating to hear later on and can be avoided by giving clear information at the beginning. Your voluntary society may publish leaflets which could help.

Give clear guidance about how your child is limited by his problems and areas where as much should be expected of him as everyone else. Make it clear whether any drugs he takes cause drowsiness or not so the teachers can tell whether poor attention is due to drugs rather than an ordinary late night or a boring lesson. (In my experience, they tend to assume it is the drugs unless you have told them otherwise.) Make sure the school know of any warning signs of impending trouble they should watch for and the action they should take. Don't assume the school doctor will have given the school any necessary medical information – many parents' find this does not happen.

If your child is to have an ancillary helper in the classroom, you will need to give more detailed advice on lifting, changing, physiotherapy exercises, etc. Remember that she, like the teachers, may be apprehensive so make sure you point out what she and your child can safely do as well as what to avoid. A conversation consisting entirely of 'Be careful not to force his legs apart' and 'If you do that you can really hurt' will not only be so discouraging she wishes she had never taken the job but also encourage her to be over-protective.

Your child's time at school will be happier if the staff understand how he feels about his difficulties. Explain if he is very sensitive about teasing on any issue like constant coughing or being incontinent. It can help minimize teasing and awkward questions if the teacher explains your child's situation to the rest of the class. Whether this should be done before he starts or later with his cooperation will depend on your individual situation and your child's character.

Incontinence causes much embarrassment among disabled children. It is a very personal problem and even young children will appreciate privacy and be reluctant for other children to know. Think back to your childhood and I am sure you will remember school toilets being very unprivate places. Even if there were locks on the doors (which there often weren't) there was often some little horror who crawled under the door or peeked over the top. Times may have changed but children have not, so your child is likely to be reluctant to deal with pads and bags in the ordinary toilets. Some schools allow the staff toilets to be used in these circumstances. These often have the added advantage of more space. If your child has pads changed by his helper, this may be done in the medical room (if there is one). Again privacy will be appreciated, so arrange for a lock on the door if none is provided.

Contact the school again a week or so after your child has started. The staff have probably thought of other questions they need answering and you will feel happier if you know everything is all right.

If things go wrong

Hopefully all will go well with your child's school career but you may be unlucky and find he is unhappy or his work is deteriorating. The big danger is to assume all problems he has at school are due to his special needs. They might be but equally well they might not. Many ordinary children have problems at school and your child is as likely as any other to find he dislikes a teacher, is bored or over-faced by the work or is being picked on and teased by another child or a teacher. It is important to take your child's problems seriously and deal with them promptly. The more entrenched the problems become, the harder they are to solve.

Obviously the first stage is to ask your child what is wrong but don't be surprised if he does not tell you, perhaps even declaring everything is fine when you can see it isn't. Many children are reluctant to admit they are being bullied or cannot do the work.

The next step is to contact the school and arrange to talk to his class teacher, head of year or headteacher, whoever seems appropriate to you. When you make the appointment, warn them why you are coming so they can look into the situation before you arrive. Often your letter or phone call will be the first sign the school have had that all is not well.

Hopefully, after they are aware a problem exists, the staff will take action to sort it out. The behaviour of teachers or other children may change or your child's day be rearranged so he has less contact with the people who upset him. More help may be given in difficult subjects and extra praise may restore shattered confidence. Your child may feel better anyway once he feels people are taking his problems seriously.

If talking to the school does not help, try contacting the education welfare officer or educational psychologist. They may talk to the school on your behalf or offer other suggestions. Some schools take difficulties with school work more seriously if an educational psychologist is involved and explains why the problems are there.

You could also contact the school governors. Their role has grown in importance in recent years as new legislation has given them increased powers and responsibilities. In particular, they have a specific responsibility to ensure that all pupils with special educational needs receive the help they require, whether they have a Statement or not. The governors may be able to back you in a disagreement with the school or support the school in its efforts to obtain the resources it needs from the education authority. They are also the right people to contact if you are unhappy because your child is being excluded from all or part of the National Curriculum.

If the situation does not improve, you may need to consider the more drastic action of changing schools. Obviously this is not something to do lightly over trivial issues but there are occasions when it is the best solution, especially if your child is so deeply unhappy it is making him ill or ruining his life. Before you request a change, visit the alternative schools so you are sure the new one will be an improvement.

Your request for a school transfer should be made to your Chief Education Officer. Provided both the new and existing heads are happy with the change and the new arrangement will not be more expensive, the transfer is likely to be granted. However, you may have to fight hard for a change to a school in another area or one run by a voluntary society because of the costs involved (see Chapter 10).

Frequent absences

Any child who is away from school loses out on contact with friends and on continuity of work. If your child is away a great deal, he may not feel properly part of the school when he is there. The other children will be in groups of friends to which he does not belong. Lessons will usually be based on work he has not done so subjects like maths may be completely incomprehensible. Not surprisingly, he can easily lose his motivation for school tasks and even grow to hate going.

If you know your child is likely to have many absences, it is important to have a good plan worked out with the school to help him cope. Work can be set for him to do at home or in hospital when he is well enough. If this is worked out carefully, he should be reasonably up-to-date when he returns. If you can persuade your LEA to provide a home tutor, her regular visits can increase your child's motivation as well as providing any necessary help.

Ideally, this plan needs to be worked out in advance, not when he has already been away for ages. It is better to have a plan just in case, even if it is never used, than to hit a bad patch of health with no help available. Frequent absences from school provide sufficient grounds to ask for a statement under the 1981 Education Act. We have found that, when the need arises, a plan formally laid down in this way works better than vague promises.

29

Helping your Child to Face the Future

Thanks to baby-sitters and school, there are times when you can return to a semblance of normal life; when you can go out without people staring and temporarily forget drugs, physiotherapy and other problems. For your child there is no such relief. For him, the problems are always there 24 hours-a-day, seven days-a-week. They cloud his future, affecting his choice of hobbies, friends and career. You cannot protect him from all the hurts life may hold nor fight all his battles for him but you can help by giving him a firm emotional base from which to face the future.

Facing facts

When one of my boys was three, he told me with great confidence, 'I have to take medicine with my food. Daddy did too when he was a little boy and when I grow up I won't need it anymore just like Daddy doesn't.' No one had ever told him that – it certainly wasn't true – it was just his way of making sense of reality as he saw it. When your child is very small, he too may assume his problems are only temporary ones which he will eventually outgrow unless you teach him otherwise.

Try to talk to your child about his condition from his earliest days (or from soon after the diagnosis) so he grows up with the knowledge he needs. Explain what is wrong in words suitable to his level of understanding and gradually expand on that basic explanation once he has understood it and wants to know more. Be prepared to repeat your explanation many times as your child is unlikely to understand and remember all the facts straightaway. There are some excellent children's books available about how the body works which can help you explain what is wrong. Also your voluntary society may produce a booklet which could help you.

It is important never to lie even though the truth may hurt. If you do lie, your child will find out eventually and will lose his trust in what you tell him in the future. However, there is no need to kill all hope completely. Many illnesses and handicapping conditions are variable in their long-term effects. There is nothing wrong in admitting you don't know what the future holds.

You may feel you want to spare him too much pain by holding back some facts about his condition until he is older, especially if his condition is progressive or terminal. Although it is sensible not to pour out all the bad news when your child is not ready to hear it, it is also wrong to hold back facts when he asks for them. Remember you are not his only source of information, especially as he gets older. Other children at school may repeat things they have heard from their parents, while television, radio and the press often carry items on handicapped or sick children and their problems. Your child may be more upset by learning painful facts through these sources than he would have been if you had told them to him gently and sympathetically.

The press, TV and radio can be particularly hurtful because, in their search for the dramatic, they frequently use words like incurable and fatal. If your child is frightened by such an item, try looking together at the way the media exaggerates other stories so he can get things in perspective. If your child has AIDS you will need to be particularly sensitive to the publicity he is likely to see.

Emotional reactions

As your child comes to realize the full impact of the problems he faces, he has every right to be upset and angry. Remembering your own reactions to the diagnosis can give you some idea of how he feels but don't fall into the trap of saying 'I know how you feel' because you don't (unless you suffer from the same disability). Having a sick or handicapped child is different from being sick or handicapped yourself.

It feels horrible if your child chooses to take out his anger on you but it is actually healthy. It shows he trusts you sufficiently to feel able to show you his true feelings. However, this does not mean you can't show him less painful and destructive ways of expressing his anger than kicking you on the shins. Digging, hammering, throwing cushions and making lots of noise can all be useful.

Your child may welcome a chance to talk about his feelings to someone outside the family, especially as he grows older and wants to be more independent. He may feel more able to talk to someone not emotionally involved as he does not have to worry about upsetting them. Asking someone else to help does not mean you have failed your child – it is just acknowledging a perfectly natural state of affairs. A more distant relative, a friend or a professional such as a doctor, teacher or social worker may take this role or you could try a child psychiatrist, psychologist or psychotherapist.

Your child may also benefit from talking to other children or adults who face similar problems. They can offer practical advice on how to cope as well as easing any feelings of isolation he may have. It is worth making an effort to arrange such contacts if they do not happen naturally through attendance at a special school. There are some holidays organized for groups of children with similar conditions which allow just such contact – ask your voluntary society or the Holiday Care Service for ideas.

Some children do not express their anger and unhappiness outwardly. Instead, they turn in upon themselves, becoming withdrawn and depressed. Although this may be easier to live with (at least at first) than a child who is kicking the walls and you, it is less healthy.

If your child finds it difficult to express his feelings because he is withdrawn and reluctant to talk about them or because he is very young or has poor communication skills, he may benefit from contact with someone trained to work with children using psycho-therapy or play therapy. She can help him express his emotions and worries using play materials instead of words. Such therapy takes time but can be very beneficial for it is easy for adults to misjudge which aspects of a child's problems are causing the greatest distress.

Conforming

Children are very conforming beings – they love to be the same as everyone else and the odd-one-out is vulnerable to teasing from the less pleasant members of the group. Your child will be very sensitive to all the aspects of his condition which make him different from other children, You cannot make him like all the others but you can do your best to minimize the differences.

Some children's desire to hide their disabilities can lead them to reject the help they need. They would rather forgo any potential benefits than be seen to be different. I have heard of children who refused to wear thick glasses or hearing aids or who would not take necessary drugs when out with friends. One disabled mother recalled how, as a teenager, she discarded her walking stick in favour of a rolled umbrella and prayed it wouldn't rain.

If your child reacts this way, understand his feelings and go along with them as far as possible. Would the family budget stretch to a fashionable pair of glasses or contact lenses (if they are suitable)? Could your doctor change the drugs to ones which are only taken once or twice a day so your child no longer needs to take them at school? Perhaps you can think of some other compromises which would make it easier for your child to accept the help he needs.

You can minimize your child's obvious differences and make it easier for him to be accepted by other children if you ensure he is dressed the same way as everyone else. Remember that does not mean the same as you were dressed at the same age. One teenager I met laughed loudly when I asked how the mentally handicapped students at our local college fitted in with the others. 'You can spot them a mile off,' he said, 'they're the only ones who look clean and smart. The boys wear ties and the girls dresses and tights while all the other students wear jeans and tatty trainers.'

If your child is not able to choose his own clothes as he grows older, enlist the help of other young people of similar ages. Mail order catalogues can also show you modern fashions. Don't assume your teenage daughter won't take pleasure in her appearance or enjoy wearing make-up just because she is handicapped or sick.

Compensating

I am sure there are some things your special child cannot do well (or perhaps at all). He may not be able to master some skills which come easily to ordinary children unless he has extra help and encouragement.

However, too much emphasis on his lack of abilities will be as depressing for him as it would be for me to have someone constantly talking about my inability to sing in tune. I am sure you too have things you cannot do well but I doubt if you would put them down first (if at all) in a list of facts about you. Like me, you would concentrate on the things you can do and encouraging your child to take the same approach will help build his self-confidence.

When my eldest son was about to change from primary to middle school, his self-confidence was at a low ebb. The only things which singled him out from his classmates was his constant cough and his small size, both results of his cystic fibrosis and neither likely to earn him respect from the other children. Then, one day he came home from school and proudly announced the teacher had told him he was the best one at standing on his head. We followed up this first glimmer of ability by encouraging him to join a gym club where he caught the enthusiasm of the other boys and the coaches. By the time he went to his new school he was not 'that short kid' or 'the boy who coughs' but 'the boy who can walk on his hands'. This rather strange ability gave his self-confidence an enormous boost he has never lost even though gym has now been replaced by other interests.

Help your child find something within his capabilities which he can do well. It will increase his self-confidence and improve his standing in the eyes of other children. If he has poor mobility, how about drawing, model making, music or computing? Even if he has quite severe learning difficulties, he may enjoy cooking, gardening or pet keeping. Many special children find it hard to excel in sports like football which require speed, good co-ordination and agility but there are other sports available which are less demanding and/or more individual. For example, you don't need to be able to walk to take part in archery and children with poor mobility on land may gain great pleasure from swimming. Horse riding can be enjoyed even by severely handicapped children (especially if you have a local group of the Riding for the Disabled Association) and learning to control such a large animal is a great confidence booster. The ideas are endless – start with your child's current interests and abilities and work from there.

Spoiling doesn't help

Because your child already has so much to cope with, it can be tempting to spoil him – to fail to demand good behaviour and to indulge him with everything he wants. Neither is a good idea. Interestingly enough, the people who asked me most strongly to pass this message on to parents were disabled young people themselves. One girl with cerebral palsy described some of the other children at her school as being very spoilt. As she explained, 'Getting everything they asked for didn't make them better people as they could not see past themselves.'

Your child will find more than normal difficulties when he comes to make his way in the world. Spoiling him now will not make it easier for him to deal with them. On the contrary, it will prevent him learning how to cope with disappointment and frustration. Life is hard enough anyway but for a spoilt child it will seem even harder.

Expect an appropriate standard of behaviour for your child's level of development and don't assume all his bad behaviour is due to his problems. Even though he is special, he is still first and foremost a child and, like any ordinary child, he can be naughty sometimes just to see what you will do. Also you are just a mother, not a saint, so don't feel you have failed if there are times when he gets on your nerves and you lose your temper.

There are probably as many theories on disciplining children as there are parents. The two main rules are, be consistent and only punish deliberate naughtiness, not clumsiness or lack of experience. The child who spills the orange squash because he is clumsy or did not understand how to screw on the lid does not need disciplining. The child who deliberately pours it on the floor to annoy you does.

Friends

Everyone is happier if they have friends and your child is no exception. You can help him meet local children before he starts school by taking him to a local mother-and-toddler group or playgroup. With some encouragement from you, friendships started then may last into school age, even if your child has to attend a special school.

Asking other children to play at your home is also a good idea. I have heard of some parents who invested in a big item like a paddling pool, climbing frame or slide to attract neighbouring children to their home thus giving their child some companionship. If your child has learning difficulties, a few games which rely completely on luck rather than skill may enable him to play with other children without automatically losing. For older children, Cubs, Brownies, Scouts and Guides can be a good source of local friendships as can your local PHAB club, if there is one.

Look around your friends and you will probably find most of them are very similar to you in lifestyle and interests. In the desire to integrate your child into ordinary life, don't overlook the possibility that he might enjoy meeting other people with similar problems. Being the only one in a group who is different can sometimes be lonely. You could consider a holiday with similar children or you may have contact with other children like yours through your voluntary society or your child's special school.

Growing up

It is natural for a child gradually to gain independence from his parents, to make his own choices and live with their consequences. This process starts in babyhood and continues throughout childhood but it accelerates in adolescence. Just because your child has problems, does not mean he won't want independence but it may make it harder for him to achieve it. Your immobile child may long for privacy as much as his able counterpart who can rush out of the kitchen and shut himself in his bedroom.

For some children, total independence may be an impossible dream but that is no reason why they should not exercise as much control over their lives as possible. Try to give your child as much freedom and responsibility as appropriate for his age and development. Even if he is very handicapped, he may be able to choose which drinks to have and which clothes to wear. Try gradually to increase his freedom of choice as he grows older.

Most parents find adolescence a difficult stage to cope with in their offspring so you should not be surprised if you do too. It is at this stage that your child may feel the full impact of the problems he will face in adult life so anger and frustration at this may be added to normal teenage moodiness.

The natural desire for independence may show itself in a refusal to accept treatment, especially if it is given by you. Tact and understanding are necessary to cope with this. Try, if you can, to avoid becoming completely at loggerheads with each other in a 'Yes, you will', 'No, I won't' argument. Acknowledge that his feelings and opinions are important and look for ways around the problem. Could he learn to carry out treatments himself or could they be done at a more convenient time or in a more private place? It can also help if you involve your child fully in discussions and decisions about his health so he fully understands the need for his treatment and feels part of the team. Remember that, unless your child's problems prevent it, there will come a time when he will take full responsibility for his own life. Then it will be entirely up to him whether he accepts the treatment he needs or not. Allowing your child gradually to become more involved in his medical care during adolescence is part of the growing up process.

Epilogue

When I began this book I felt it was important to tackle all the sources of emotional strain parents encounter. There is one field I have avoided so far but which I believe I must include – the spiritual side of life. If your religious belief or your atheism is so strong it can withstand any stress, you have no need of this chapter. I am writing for the people like me who find their child's problems bring them face to face with the deeper questions of life: Why is there sickness? Why my child? Where is God in all this?

I find I cannot write this chapter without reference to my own Christian belief. If your religious background is different from mine, I hope you can adjust my words to your need and still find benefit from them.

Why?

I don't know why the world is not a perfect place. Some people believe the story of Adam and Eve and explain that all the suffering in the world is due to man's imperfections. Certainly no supernatural force prevents us from drinking and driving or polluting our environment – so many of our problems really are caused by ourselves. However, it is harder to explain the existence of crippling diseases or huge disasters like earthquakes.

Whatever the reason, the world is as it is – far from perfect. I believe that illness and suffering are symptoms of the world's imperfections rather than of our own. Look around you – there is no fairness to the distribution of problems. The righteous and the good have as many as everyone else.

As dwellers on this planet, we have no more right to expect freedom from all problems than the next man. Praying to God is not a religious antibiotic which protects us from all known germs. Being religious is not a passport to an easy life nor does going to church every Sunday protect us from being run over by a bus. However, although faith does not protect us, it can help us to cope and become better rather than bitter people.

I cannot answer your 'Why?' any more than you can. Personally, I put the question aside now, accepting that the answer is beyond

145

my comprehension. For me, it is important to look for good coming out of the bad; to see what can happen now rather than what might have been. Some other parents are greatly helped by feeling chosen by God to care for their special child. Whatever explanation gives you peace is the right one for you. I hope you will find it soon.

Spiritual healing

A major part of Jesus' ministry was healing the sick and healing has been part of the work of the Church ever since. Although its importance lessened over the centuries, there has been a great revival in the healing ministry during recent years. Even if you do not think of the idea yourself, someone is likely to suggest that you pray for your child to be healed.

Healing does not have to mean a miracle. God can also work slowly through the doctors, teachers and other people who are trying to help your child. Sometimes healing can be of inner feelings rather than a total cure, giving you and your child the courage and the peace you need to cope with what the future holds.

One mother told me how she believes God prevents her ever being less than gentle with her profoundly handicapped daughter by placing an invisible net of protection around the child. This same mother had also seen slight but noticeable improvements in her daughter since a prayer group had prayed for her regularly. She is only one of many parents, including myself, who feel prayer (both their own and other people's) has helped both them and their children.

When healing does not happen

It is very painful to pray for healing but see no result. You have put your trust in God but nothing has happened. Some teaching about healing makes this pain worse by blaming you. It declares that God will heal anyone who asks him provided they do it properly so if healing does not happen, it is not God's fault but yours. You have some unrepented sin in your life, your faith is too weak or you failed to claim the healing properly.

I am sure that these hurtful ideas are wrong. God is not a computer who must do what we want if we press the right buttons. He is wiser than us and we only get what we pray for if he feels it is right, if it is according to his will. Although he may not choose to interfere with the world by freeing us from our problems, that does not mean he is unwilling to support us through our difficulties.

Where is God in all this?

Anger is a natural reaction when things go wrong. If you believe in God at all, you have probably felt angry with him for your child's problems, for letting you down when you trusted him to look after you. Don't worry: having a good grumble at God does not condemn you for the rest of your life. Faith can survive such bad times and even be strengthened by them.

I believe God is there beside you. He cares about you and wants to help even when you are so low you don't know he exists. He persuaded me to write this book, made me keep going when I felt like giving up, taught me to learn from my own mistakes and showed me which topics were most important. I hope it has helped you – if it has, he's the one to thank.

Appendix A
Useful Addresses

ACE – The Advisory Centre for Education
18 Victoria Park Square
London E2 9PB
Tel. 01 980 4596

Across Trust
Bridge House
70/72 Bridge Road
East Molesley
Surrey KT8 9HF
Tel. 01 783 1355

Organizes pilgrimages to Lourdes and other holidays.

Action for Victims of Medical Accidents
Bank Chambers
1 London Road
London SE23 3TP
Tel. 01 291 2793

AFASIC – The Association for all Speech Impaired Children
347 Central Markets
London EC1A 9NH
Tel. 01 236 3632/6487

ASBAH – Association for Spina Bifida and Hydrocephalus
ASBAH House
42 Park Road
Peterborough PE1 2UQ
Tel. 0733 555 988

The British Heart Foundation
102 Gloucester Place
London W1H 4DH
Tel. 01 935 0185

The British Kidney Patient Association
Bordon
Hants
Tel. 042 032021/2

The Brittle Bone Society
Unit 4
Block 20
Carlunie Road
Dundee DD2 3QT
Tel. 0382 817771

The Carers' National Association
29 Chilworth Mews
London W2 3RG
Tel. 01 724 7776

The Children's Legal Centre
20 Compton Terrace
London N1 2UN
Tel. 01 359 6251

Provides a free advice and information service.

Cleft Lip and Palate Association
The Hospital for Sick Children, Great Ormond Street
London WC1N 3JH
Tel. 01 405 9200

The Compassionate Friends
6 Denmark Street
Bristol BS1 5DQ
Tel. 0272 292778

Offers support to bereaved parents.

Contact a Family
16 Strutton Ground
London SW1P 2HP
Tel. 01 222 2695

Links parents of sick or handicapped children to other families with
similar problems.

Cystic Fibrosis Research Trust
Alexandra House
5 Blyth Road
Bromley
Kent BR1 3RS
Tel. 01 464 7211

Disabled Living Foundation
380–384 Harrow Road
London W9 2HU
Tel. 01 289 6111

Down's Children Association
12/13 Clapham Common Southside
London SW4 7AA
Tel. 01 720 0008

The Family Fund
PO Box 50
York Y01 1UY

Provides financial help for families caring for a severely handicapped child.

Friedreich's Ataxia Group
Copse Edge
Thursley Road
Elstead
Godingham
Surrey GR8 6DJ
Tel. 0252 702864

Handicapped Children's Pilgrimage Trust
100A High Street
Banstead
Surrey SM7 2RB
Tel. 0737 353311

The Haemophilia Society
123 Westminster Bridge Road
London SE1 7HR
Tel. 01 928 2020

USEFUL ADDRESSES

Helen House
37 Leopold Street
Oxford OX4 1QT
Tel. 0865 728251

Holiday Care Service
2 Old Bank Chambers
Station Road
Horley
Surrey RH6 9HW
Tel. 0293 774535

ICAN – Invalid Children's Aid Nationwide
Allen Graham House
198 City Road
London EC1V 2PH
Tel. 01 608 2462

Independent Panel of Special Education Experts
Administrator – John Wright
12 Marsh Road
Tillingham
Essex CM10 7SZ
Tel. 0621 87781

'In Touch'
10 Norman Road
Sale
Cheshire M33 3DF

A newsletter for parents which links together families whose children have similar problems.

Leukaemia Research Fund
43 Great Ormond Street
London WC1N 3JJ
Tel. 01 405 0101

Martin House
Grove Road
Clifford
West Yorks LS23 6TX
Tel. 0937 845045

MENCAP – Royal Society for Mentally Handicapped Children and Adults
MENCAP National Centre
123 Golden Lane
London EC1Y ORT
Tel. 01 253 9433

Muscular Dystrophy Group of Great Britain and Northern Ireland
Nattrass House
35 Macaulay Road
London SW4 OQP
Tel. 01 720 8055

National Association for the Welfare of Children in Hospital
Argyle House
29–31 Euston Road
London NW1 2SD
Tel. 01 833 2041

National Autistic Society
276 Willesden Lane
London NW2
Tel. 01 451 1114

National Children's Bureau
8 Wakley Street
London EC1V 7QE
Tel. 01 278 9441

Connected with the Voluntary Council for Handicapped Children who are at the same address.

The National Deaf Children's Society
45 Hereford Road
London W2 5AH
Tel. 01 229 9272/4

National Fostercare Association
Francis House
Francis Street
London SW1P 1DE
Tel. 01 828 6266

Network '81
Southern England
52 Magnaville Road
Bishops Stortford
Herts CM33 4DW
Tel. 0279 503244

Northern England
112 Grove Park
Knutsford
Cheshire WA16 8QD
Tel. 0565 2666

Network for the Handicapped
The Secretary
16 Princeton Street
London WC1R 4BB
Tel. 01 831 8031/7740

A law and advisory centre for handicapped people and their families.

Parents Anonymous (London)
9 Manor Gardens
London N7 6LA
Tel. 01 263 5672/8918

A group for parents under stress.

Parentline–OPUS
106 Godstone Road
Whyteleafe
Surrey CR3 OEB
Tel. 01 645 0469

An organization for any parents under stress.

Parents Lifeline
Station House
73D Stapleton Hall Road
London N4 3QF
Tel. 01 263 2265

Crisis support for parents with seriously ill children in hospital.

PHAB
Tavistock House North
Tavistock Square
London WC1H 9HX ·
Tel. 01 388 1963

Runs clubs for physically handicapped and able-bodied children.

PLAYMATTERS
The National Toy Libraries Association
68 Churchway
London NW1 1LT
Tel. 01 387 9592

PPIAS – Parent for Parent Information on Adoption Services
Lower Boddington
Daventry
Northamptonshire NN11 6YB
Tel. 0327 60295

RADAR – Royal Association for Disability and Rehabilitation
25 Mortimer Street
London W1N 8AB
Tel. 01 637 5400

Research Trust for Metabolic Diseases in Children
53 Beam Street
Nantwich
Cheshire CW5 5NF
Tel. 0270 629782/626834

Riding for the Disabled Association
Avenue 'R'
National Agricultural Centre
Kenilworth
Warwicks CV8 2LY
Tel. 0203 696510

Scottish Council for Spastics
22 Corstorphine Road
Edinburgh EH12 6HP
Tel. 031 337 9876

Scottish Society for the Mentally Handicapped
13 Elmbank Street
Glasgow G2 4QA
Tel. 041 226 4541

Scottish Spina Bifida Association
190 Queensferry Road
Edinburgh EH4 2BW
Tel. 031 332 0743

SENSE – National Association for Deaf-Blind and Rubella Handicapped
311 Gray's Inn Road
London WC1X 8PT
Tel. 01 278 1005/1000

The Society for Mucopolysaccharide Diseases
30 Westwood Drive
Little Chalfont
Bucks
Tel. 02404 2789

The Spastics Society
12 Park Crescent
London W1N 4EQ
Tel. 01 636 5020

Appendix B
Further Reading

Dr Vernon Coleman *How to Stop Feeling Guilty*.
  Sheldon Press 1982
Disability Rights Handbook.
  Published annually by The Disability Alliance, and available
  directly from them at 25 Denmark Street, London WC2H 8NJ
James Dobson *Hide or Seek*. Hodder and Stoughton 1982
  How to build confidence in your child.
Dr Peter Hanson *The Joy of Stress*. Pan 1987
  Good, sensible advice given in a light-hearted easy style.
Pat King *How do You Find the Time?*
  Pickering and Ingliss 1982
  Ideas on time management from a Christian mother of ten.
Elisabeth Kubler-Ross *On Children and Death*.
  Macmillan 1983
  The best book I have seen on the subject.
Gerald Sanctuary *After I'm Gone – What Will Happen to my
  Handicapped Child?* Souvenir Press 1984
Peter Newell *ACE Special Education Handbook*.
  Advisory Centre for Education 1988
  Available directly from ACE.

Index